Praise for *Risking the Rapids*

"For many years now, the poet, playwright, and memoirist Irene O'Garden has been a hero to me. I think of her as a walking, writing, beam of light. It is my hope that...numberless others will come to know her gifts, and most of all, her captivating talent for wonder and marvel."
—Elizabeth Gilbert, author of *Eat, Pray, Love* and *Big Magic*

"*Risking the Rapids* is a deep and powerful memoir. Irene O'Garden sifts through her family's shared pain (and shared joy!) with elegance and care—searching for nothing less than ultimate understanding and supreme forgiveness."
—Martha Beck, sociologist, life coach, bestselling author, columnist for *O Magazine*

"Set aside a goodly few hours with O'Garden's enthralling memoir and plunge into the lives of a family that has chosen you as their new member. Here they are on horseback, immersed in rivers, on tops of mountains—camping, sleeping, quarreling, and forgiving ... *Risking the Rapids* embraces our being and never lets go."
—Malachy McCourt, author of *Ireland* and *A Monk Swimming*

" 'Family is landscape,' writes Irene O'Garden in her breathtaking memoir, *Risking the Rapids*. She gives us a bold dose of both as she embarks on a remote river trip to help make sense of a family wild and dangerous. In her brave eloquence, O'Garden adds a thoroughly welcome voice to the rich vein of American literature on the singular healing powers of wilderness."
—Florence Williams, author of *The Nature Fix*, *LA Times* Book Prize winner, and editor at *Outside Magazine*

"It is a tricky business, navigating the river of forgiveness while honoring the injured self. In that wilderness, the psyche must surrender to each boulder life smashes it against, and then it must stand in awe as we experience the changes wrought within our very DNA that are the gifts of facing down our demons; the gifts of looking our inner and outer truths square in the eye. O'Garden does this better than anyone I know and then puts it into words that have the cadence of angels."

—Linda Ford Blaikie, CSW, psychotherapist, author of Godless Grace

"Irene O'Garden's memoir is riveting, fiercely honest, and graced with poetic insight. An imaginative child plagued by insecurities, O'Garden vied with six siblings for her parents' approval and lived beneath the Damoclean sword of Catholic doctrine. Her chronicle of growing up in what seemed then a normal Midwestern family in the 1950s and '60s asks, 'Who were we, really?' in a far-ranging, haunting journey of discovery."

—Victoria Riskin, former president, Writers Guild of America, West, author of Fay Wray and Robert Riskin: A Hollywood Memoir

"Irene O'Garden's *Risking the Rapids* is, simply put, a literary triumph. Her roiling journey through the whitewater of big family turbulence is alternately a companionable sisterly punch in the shoulder and a vicious left hook to the jaw. And as is true for all superb writing, it is the 'left hook' that unexpectedly provides the narrator's stunning— even transcendent—passage into calm waters and healing. Put aside whatever has gained your attention right now and read this book. O'Garden is truly a wonderful guide."

—Steven Lewis, New York Times writer, Sarah Lawrence Writing Institute teacher, author of Loving Violet

"*Risking the Rapids* artfully peels back the layers of family to reveal both the darkness and the diamond. O'Garden lyrically shares the challenging circumstances of her Midwest Catholic childhood as a thread woven through a story of present-day danger during what is supposed to be a simple outing. The kaleidoscope effect of past and present, reflection and struggle, brings the reader along on a powerful healing journey to bring what is hidden into the light."

—**HeatherAsh Amara, author of *Warrior Goddess Training***

"I haven't experienced this kind of reverberating tension and utter fascination with a family since Jeannette Walls's memoir, *The Glass Castle*. Irene O'Garden's long career of treasured work hits its highest note yet with her memoir. How she survived her upbringing in a big, dysfunctional Catholic family—and the harrowing wilderness trip through white waters she took as an adult with her family—is riveting and ultimately healing."

—**Debbie Phillips, author of *Women on Fire: 20 Inspiring Women Share Their Life Secrets (and Save You Years of Struggle!)***

"Irene O'Garden is, quite frankly, the most amazing writer I know. She's a poet—just read her words aloud. She's a storyteller—consider the arc of the tale she tells here. She's a dramatist—we're in that boat with her, risking the rapids, and hopefully rescuing our past self as she so magnificently succeeds in doing."

—**John Leonard Pielmeier, author of *Hook's Tale* and *Agnes of God***

"Irene O'Garden's *Risking the Rapids* is both a meditation and a thrill ride in which a sibling's death prompts an unlikely family rafting journey through Montana's wilderness. The beauty, moods, and menace of the swollen Flathead River seem an allegory of family life, and like sunlight glinting off water, her brutally honest reckoning is told in sparkling, luminous prose that gives memoir itself a fresh new shape."

—**Edward McCann, founder and editor, Read650.com**

"*Risking the Rapids* is a sensitive depiction of a family's attempt to heal. In the tradition of classic memoirs like *The Glass Castle* that highlight the coexistence of tortured love and unresolved misery, Irene O'Garden has captured the essence of family connections. With suspense and uncertainty about how complicated relationships unfold, this story intrigues and inspires us. I highly recommend this book to all of us who struggle with the legacies of abuse and with having the hopefulness to heal."

—Sonya Rhodes, PhD, author and family therapist

Praise for Irene O'Garden's Work

"Bewitching...astounding...heartbreaking."
—*The New York Times*

"An immersion into what we relish and how we live, a kind of shining beacon that doesn't shy away from the tough stuff... Highly recommended."
—Janet Pierson, Producer, SXSW Film Conference and Festival

"In a far-ranging and elegant suite of poems, Irene O'Garden balances a galaxy of incommensurates on the fulcrum of a disciplined intelligence. 'I am a blueprint of a holy universe' seesaws against 'I feel like a set of china'—the former in a Herbert-like sacred meditation, the latter in a narrative about being chased by a bull. Her technique suggests influences ranging from Donne to Bishop, from Frost to Moore. Soulful and rewarding, these poems remind us that 'We're not made of matter but of mattering.' "
—T.R. Hummer, whose poems appear in *The New Yorker*, *Best of American Poetry*, *Harper's*, *Atlantic Monthly*, *Paris Review*, and twelve volumes of his own

"The poems in Irene O'Garden's book, *Fulcrum*, illustrate the importance and vitality of poetry in our daily lives. Beautiful imagery, powerful emotions, simplicity, complexity and thought-provoking subjects—all drawn from relatable life experiences—make reading her work a journey of discovery and reflection focusing on what it means to live a life of passion and wonderment. Like the author herself, the poems in these pages inspire and draw one in. It is a beautiful collection."
—Professor Jane Kinney-Denning of Pace University, President of Women's National Book Association

RISKING
THE
RAPIDS

Published by Mango Publishing Group, a division of Mango Media Inc.

Cover: Morgane Leoni
Layout & Design: Roberto Nunez

Author photo: Mark Lacko
Picture of Jim and Irene with bottle: Ro O'Brien
Photo of Irene leaning on sign: Ro O'Brien
Photo of Ro and Irene: Mark Muenster

For permission requests, please contact the publisher at:

Mango Publishing Group
2850 Douglas Road, 2nd Floor
Coral Gables, FL 33134 U.S.A.
info@mango.bz

For special orders, quantity sales, course adoptions and corporate sales, please email the publisher at sales@mango.bz. For trade and wholesale sales, please contact Ingram Publisher Services at customer.service@ingramcontent.com or +1.800.509.4887.

Risking the Rapids: How My Wilderness Adventure Healed My Childhood

Library of Congress Cataloging
ISBN: (p) 978-1-63353-887-0, (e) 978-1-63353-886-3
Library of Congress Control Number: 2018962580
BISAC—BIO026000—BIOGRAPHY & AUTOBIOGRAPHY / Personal Memoirs

Printed in the United States of America.

Please note: Some names and identifying details have been changed to protect the privacy of individuals.

RISKING THE RAPIDS

How My Wilderness Adventure Healed My Childhood

Irene O'Garden

Mango Publishing

CORAL GABLES, FL

God Bless
Mommy, Daddy,
Kako, Pogo, Tommy,
Skip, Irene, Jim, Rosemary,
and the Little One We Lost.

Also, all the wonderful people
preceding, married to, and descending from them.

Table of Contents

Panorama   15

Tangletown, Midcentury   17

Montana 2014, Day One: Loading Up   20

The Oaken Field   24

Long Live the Milkman   25

Within These Walls   29

Montana, Day One: Tenting Tonight   39

The Family Journal   43

Montana, Day Two: Practice   56

Between the Lines   59

A Crystal Cave   61

Twinkles   67

Montana Day Three: Angels on Horseback   69

Shifting Sands   74

Into the Spotlight   76

Fatherland   78

The Old Pew   84

Montana, Day Four: On the Raft   88

Burglar   97

Family Portrait   101

Up to the Lake   103

In the Car   104

At the Lake   105

The Hook in the Heart   106

Lake Ways   107

Montana, Day Five: In Camp   110

A Blur of Sins   114

Good Grooming   119

The Cart   123

Very Personally Yours   125

Not Normal   130

Exposure   132

The Living Water   133

Montana, Day Five: Beach Eats   135

Creating My Own Reality   138

Renovation   142

Motherland   147

At Gobby's Knee   150

Vigils   154

Montana, Day Five: That Sound   157

Rocky Terrain   159

A Nameless Night   161

Dad's Plaid   168

Gibraltar Topples   171

Montana, Day Six: Focus   176

Sibland   177

Measures Taken   178

Mercury   182

The Determined Empty Chair   185

Maladroit   188

Montana, Day Six: Aiming for Hazards   190

Ravine   192

Curious Old Path   195

Montana, Day Six: Curdles and Limits   197

Between Here and Heaven   201

Montana, Day Six: Inclinations   207

Wills Read and Written   212

Montana, Day Seven: Bequests   215

Thanksgiving 2013   220

Piecing Together   226

Montana, Day Eight: No Second Chance   232

Gifts of Family   241

Anniversary   242

Panorama's Edge   243

Acknowledgments   **246**

About the Author   **250**

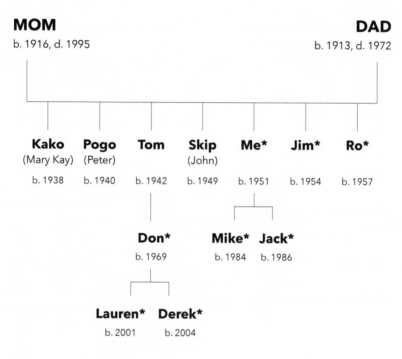

MOM
b. 1916, d. 1995

DAD
b. 1913, d. 1972

Kako
(Mary Kay)
b. 1938

Pogo
(Peter)
b. 1940

Tom
b. 1942

Skip
(John)
b. 1949

Me*
b. 1951

Jim*
b. 1954

Ro*
b. 1957

Don*
b. 1969

Mike*
b. 1984

Jack*
b. 1986

Lauren*
b. 2001

Derek*
b. 2004

* Family members on Montana trip
(Domenic, Don's nephew by marriage, also on trip)

Panorama

Most of my siblings are here. One by one we'll take the oath and testify. We hate to do this, but we have to be here. And we have to speak.

I am sick to my stomach. Who wants to say words that lead to locking up a loved brother? But his behavior has become...so bizarre.

How did we come to this?

Weren't we just a simple big old-fashioned Catholic family? A mom, a dad, seven kids, a Midwest city. Most of us grown up out of the fifties into the sixties. Sorta normal, right?

They call my name. What will I say? My testimony will be the most urgent. I'll have to describe his recent strange demeanor, how frightened I was at his hands. We say this is for "his good." Is it?

Years later when my sister calls to tell me John has died, these are the memories that savage.

•••

I was born in the middle. In the middle of seven children, in a mid-size city in the middle of the country, in the middle class, in the middle of the twentieth century. In a leafy neighborhood neither urban nor suburban. In the middle of surprising anxieties, given the idyllic qualities a mid-century childhood afforded: freedom, autonomy, solitude.

Our parents never beat us. We had enough to eat and wear. But one brother cut all his pictures out of the family scrapbook. Another brother: committed to a madhouse. Another: hamstrung in hierarchy; another: crippled by pain. One sister suffered and drank, one sister trembled in fear. I ate myself upwards of two hundred pounds. What happened to us?

•••

A family is a landscape of its own, as granted as the earth and trees.

Each person, each event becomes environment, familiar, dear, and scary. Emotion is the weather of the family, patterning the faces, the voices, and the hearts.

A family is a landscape changing scope and light and season. One day the father is a mountain peak sheltering a gentle mother river, and the next the father is a fallen pine by a dried riverbed and scattered children rocks.

Dad worked in landslides; Mom in abrasion, erosion. Either way, trees fall.

A family is a landscape, not a house. Houses are intentional—everything picked, planned, placed. Chosen for a reason. A house is what a parent wants to teach a child. Nothing unexpected included.

But a family will spill and charge and go its growing way, resist attempts to still it, clip it, and capture it. Shoots grow into wild events in even the serenest grove when bent against the nature of the plant.

•••

My brother John's death prompted more than a trip to his memorial service. It impelled a journey through Montana's living wilderness with other family members and an inner passage through the landscape of family itself.

Tangletown, Midcentury

Traveling north on 35W, we could see downtown Minneapolis spring up from the plains like a spread in a pop-up book. Our family emerged from stability itself: the wide flat plains of the upper Midwest, and the level terrain of our parents' "'til death-did-them-part" marriage.

To a child's eye: a shimmering blue Emerald City. The sturdy Curtis Hotel, the Foshay Tower, shaped just like the Empire State Building; later, the IDS rising up, a *real* skyscraper. Minneapolis. An oasis of lakes and forward thinking. Why, in 1958, the first indoor shopping mall was invented and built here. In 1963, one of the first regional repertory theatres was started by Tyrone Guthrie. Five years later, downtown's main street, Nicollet, would be planted with trees and closed to automobiles—a radical, internationally-noted and imitated innovation: the Pedestrian Mall. An I.M. Pei building would anchor it. In a few more years, Mary Tyler Moore would toss her hat here. How right she was.

Downtown. The magical place you went when Mom was in a good mood. Step on the wooden shoe-sizer, get your stocking-foot measured, Buster Browns or bump-toed blue Keds to try on, march up and down the little you-sized staircase, hear the jangly *snick-snack* of Mom's charge-a-plate, then eat plush coconut marshmallows on the cab ride home.

(Unless she bought you the horrible brown Oxfords, which looked like corrective shoes and all the kids would laugh, but why did she do it and make you wear them? Your feet were okay.)

They called them "The Twin Cities," but they never seemed Twin to us—Minneapolis all silver, blue, shiny; St. Paul all dark brown, old wood, like our old confessionals before they built the new church.

Our neighborhood was known as Tangletown. Unlike the orderly elm-lined avenues of the rest of Minneapolis, these streets meandered any which way. Minnehaha Creek, not a grid-minded city planner, had laid the houses out herself, around curves and slopes—precious terrain in Flatland. Pretty, but people had a hard time finding us.

Ours was a smallish lot right on a curve. The front yard was Dad's hope for a lawn, scruffy until he banished play to the back yard. A few towering black-barked oaks and a "please don't strip that" beloved paper birch tree with its fascinating white curls blessed the front yard, as well as a trio of hemlocks outside my bedroom window which scattered the streetlight across my walls at night. A couple scrubby peonies and a foundation planting of juniper struggled in front of the sunroom, and oddly placed near the public sidewalk grew a clump of barberry. Within its hollow, I founded the short-lived Prickerbush Club, consisting of me and my neighbor girl, Cindy Massenger. We held meetings when John had meetings of the club he wouldn't let us join. Since exclusivity was our raison d'être and the prickers hurt, we swiftly disbanded.

On the north, we were close enough to read the fine print on a neighbor's cereal box. To the south was a wider shrubby side yard which protected Mr. Massenger's dahlias from our scuffling Keds. Best of all, right across the street from our front door was an almost private wilderness: the green effusion along Minnehaha Creek. The outdoors we could never wait to get to, the outdoors that took us to school and to Mass, took me away from the clamor and chaos of six other scrambling siblings.

The funny old barn-shape of our house always embarrassed me. It was a 1924 Dutch Colonial—a perfectly acceptable architectural style—but it sure didn't resemble the pointy-roof houses around us or in picture books. Just one of the ways our family wasn't like others. Ours was the only mother who didn't drive. She said she was nervous "propelling two tons of steel down an avenue," failed her test three times, and from then on was chauffeured—by Dad, bridge club friends, the trusty yellow cab company, eventually the Olders, and subsequently the Youngers.

(The continental divide between the Olders and the Youngers was The Little One We Lost. Born prematurely, Joseph died at nine hours old, nearly taking Mom with him. Mom told us later she was mad the doctors brought her back. "It was so beautiful. I was leaping from mountaintop to mountaintop." Her glimpse of afterlife has stayed with us all. Against her doctor's advice, she later gave birth to John, me, Jim and Ro.)

Clad in white clapboards and dark green shutters, the house sported green and taxi-gold striped awnings in the summer, eye-pleasing till they grew tattered. One day they were gone and never replaced.

If it's fall, Pogo and Tom are horsing around with sloppy soap and squeegees to the rise and fall of the play-by-play of the Golden Gopher college football game. While they wash and put up the tricky storm windows, we Youngers are raking, jumping in and burning the leaves, the blue-smoke smell dear and elusive, like memory itself.

No need to use the brass knocker with the little peep-door in it (The Wizard Is In!) Come in, hang your coat in the little closet. Or throw it on the couch with ours. Mom's at a luncheon anyway.

There's Copper Jesus, hanging on His Cross hanging on the wall. So sad. Then Palm Sunday fronds crisp like cornflakes behind Father Dudley's house blessing. We're lucky to have priests to help us renounce Satan, who tries to get us if he can. On the table below, monkey-pod pineapple holding rosaries, bobby pins, Monopoly top hat, and never-used keys to our never-locked doors.

This is my staircase I flew up and down. Really *flew*. It's my first memory. Then again and again, which I wish I could teach you. But no one believed me. So I forgot how. Even watching Peter Pan, I never can fly to Neverland.

Montana 2014, Day
One: Loading Up

My little brother Jim found his Neverland thirty years ago in
Montana's Bob Marshall Wilderness. It's the zenith of his year to mount
a horse and head in with a son or two, a nephew, good friends and
good whiskey.

After our brother John dies in February, Jim invites me and Ro
to join him in July, which is how I ended up here in the parking lot of
my Missoula hotel, hunk by chunk, hoisting with his boys a circus of
duffels, backpacks, stuff sacks, tubs, coolers, and the deadweight of two
folded hundred-pound river rafts into a rusting trailer hitched to his son
Mike's SUV.

Day after tomorrow, we'll drop it all at the outfitters. They'll bundle
and strap it on mules, pack it thirty-two miles into "The Bob," pile it
on a distant rocky beach where we'll retrieve it after our own day-long
horseback ride. Hooves are the only way to get to the South Fork of
the Flathead River. The most remote place in the lower forty-eight. My
heart rate is rising from more than exertion. I'm really going to camp
seven nights in wilderness? Thank heavens for both those Girl Scout
overnights. Maneuver a river raft? Lucky I had that hour on an inner
tube on the Delaware.

Why am I doing this? Threat holds no appeal for me. I sit out high-
risk stuff—skydiving, rock climbing, downhill skiing—I had enough
scares growing up, thank you. I want my life to pass before my eyes just
that once, when it's supposed to, right there at the end.

"This is not that," Jim had assured me. He could hardly be more
different than my brother John. Both railed against bullies, but
Jim's never been one. He fights them in court. Puffy-eyed and hawk-
nosed from poring over depositions and briefs, building cases for the
underdog—medical malpractice, workman's comp, domestic violence—

his is the kind, fervent face of a saint carved into medieval stone, and his manner could coax a cat out of a creamery.

"It's a *float*, not a raft trip. River's low, end of July. Glide through the spectacular country. Water so clear you could cry. Rock gardens. I'll teach you fly fishing. It's so remote the fish practically come up and shake your hand."

Sumptuous visions of "A River Runs Through It" arise, but the real allure runs deeper. Whenever he talks about the backcountry, Jim's eyes sparkle like wet agate. I'll never really know my dear loquacious brother unless I go "back" with him. I'm sixty-two, he's sixty. John died at sixty-five. If not now, when?

And consider the rest of the intrepid band: our beloved little sister Ro (love being with her), Jim's grown sons Mike and Jack, our brother Tom's son Don, with his two kids and their cousin—all people I want to know better. All kind hearts with good senses of humor. And everybody else has loads of wilderness experience. The beauty. The challenge. The family. Why not?

Had I known all this trip would entail—the blood, the tears, the horror—would I have said yes?

•••

In the hotel parking lot, Jim instructs me to "fine-tooth-comb" my suitcase.

Good Boomer that I am, I've procured the right equipment: well-made sunglasses, wicking shirts, pants that zip to shorts. Teeny travel towel. Compressible pillow. All-purpose camp soap to wash hair, self, dishes and laundry. Oh, and a tiny set of watercolors for idle hours. Only thing New York couldn't provide was the mysterious item "bear spray."

"Eliminate anything unnecessary. Rest goes in this dry bag," he says, holding out one of the ostensibly waterproof nylon bags in which all belongings will be secured.

"I'll leave my lipstick, but everything else was on your packing list. Except you forgot towels. I got this."

I produce my handy little foldable quick-dry towel.

"We have towels, you won't need it."

"But it folds into nothing."

"Nah, you don't need it. Or that—we have plenty of bug spray. Leave the pillow, just use your sweater."

"Oh." My crest falls a bit. Okay. Rough it, girl.

•••

All loaded up, we breakfast at The Stone of Accord, an Irish restaurant. According to legend, ancients sealed their contracts, marriages, and other agreements by shaking hands through a hole at the top of the freestanding stone. We grip and grin through their replica.

Full of pancakes, laughter, and accord, we drive to the trailhead, where we'll meet up with Ro, camp for the night, and head out at daybreak on horses.

Holland Lake shimmers at the foot of the Swan Range, a wing of the Rockies. Situated on the shore, the campground has a Pledge-of-Allegiance view. Three states of matter—lake, mountain, and sky—adjoin so harmoniously your hand almost springs to your heart.

But when we arrive, a bony old Percy-Kilbride caretaker tells us tonight all the campsites are full.

Our vehicles slink from the campground, tailpipes between our wheels. Shoulda reserved. But we spot a parking lot below a small hill. This'll do. We haul essentials up and make camp in the long grasses under the trees. It's a ways to walk for water and the last restrooms we'll enjoy for a week, but up here no neighbor's playlist or clatter on macadam intrudes. Even the Ponderosas sigh.

I decide to walk to the lake. I emerge from the evergreens to behold, as if dropped from the clouds, my beloved sister gazing at the water. Framed by soft turquoise waves, her slender form sways ever so slightly on the pebbly shore. Sweet flash of the best of our childhood: up at the lake.

Whoops, hollers, huge hugs. Those deep, familiar, kind, kind eyes. That delicate skin, her blunt cut dashed with chestnut. People mistake her for Diane Keaton, not only because of her looks. By nature, Ro shares that delightful "La-di-da" quality and those self-effacing, syncopated cadences.

After a quick catch-up, we fall silent, staring up in admiration and fear at a big fissure in the glorious mountain.

"I think that's our horse trail tomorrow," I venture. How much of what Jim told me should I tell her? Eight hours in the saddle. Trail broiling in the open sun, slippery with scree. Horses might shy. We'll be sore for two days. But she's talked to him herself.

"He told me there's a sheer drop-off on one side. We might get frightened and light-headed. Have to dismount and walk. The guide might not even stop to let us pee. They just keep going. He said we only get one little water bottle apiece, to keep the saddlebags light."

"I'm not giving up my chamois cream! I googled saddle sores. It's what professional bike racers use. But you know how bad I am when I'm dehydrated."

"God, I hope we're up to this." We look at each other and scream. "Aaaahhhh!" Then laugh.

"But this time tomorrow the worst of our trip will be over, right?"

"Jim says we'll just float and fish and read. Right?"

Returning to camp, Ro and I are touched to discover our considerate nephew Don not only packed sleeping bags and air mattresses for both of us, he brought and erected "Big Agnes," a peachy little two-person tent. His aunties will have shelter and privacy in the wild.

What a great guy! Thoughtful, always willing to help. And that sweet open face—if you look fast and slap on a mental mustache, why, it could almost be my Dad's.

The Oaken Field

In his early fan photos, Dad could have passed for Clark Gable's less rakish, undimpled brother: same dark hair, generous brow, mustache. And he wasn't even on camera yet.

Here in our '50s dining room, he presided at our long, heavy, Spanishly-dark oak refectory table, curly swerves carved into the massive ball feet and the matching chair backs. If our family were a piece of furniture, it would be this weighty, battered, accommodating, honest table. The most stimulating, philosophical, and entertaining conversations took place here; later, some of the most traumatic.

The grand rambunctious parliament of dinner: huge table, edged with eager us, tipping in the carven chairs, yearning to tell what we learned in school, to ignite some grand discussion, to contribute to it, make some rare, insightful point: to solve the very sound of the tree falling by itself in the forest.

Get the dictionary! Look it up! Semantics! Standard English! And always, if we talked enough, we'd come to the Nature of God.

A stone too heavy for us to lift. But we would try, as surely as we'd try to lick our elbows for the hundred dollars Dad promised on nonsense nights when we played The Rhyming Game, or Puck, a hockey of the hands with a milkbottle cap, or Dad made Clown Sundaes, or told funny stories, or invented games, word games, games of love, Mom laughing and abashed, proud and alarmed at her brood. In the best of times.

Which is where we will start.

With the December night in 1952, Dad hatched a clever way to teach us table manners. (We have it in writing.) I like to imagine how it came about.

Long Live the Milkman

The swinging dining room door squeaks on its hinges and through it comes pudgy fourteen-year-old Mary Kay in snug, flour-dusty dungarees. Her hair—a clumsy-curled banister-brown page boy—hangs limply, and her pointy black cat-eye glasses are slipping down her nose. She lugs the ungainly half-gallon glass bottle of milk as if it were a baby on her hip and fills each bright aluminum tumbler.

"Everybody wash your ha-yands," she calls. No response. "Pineapple cake for dessert," she adds. Pogo, twelve, and Tom, ten, thunder down the stairs, muscling into the tiny half-bath, grinding powdery Borax hand soap into their dirty-from-dirt hands. Three-year-old Skip (John's childhood nickname) tries to nudge his way in. I'm ready to go into my high chair.

With one small reddened bird-ish hand, Mom plucks up her Pall Mall, takes a drag, stubs it out on discolored melamine. She hefts the boiling stockpot to the sink and dumps it, draining the egg noodles, then coats them in margarine and poppy seeds. One delicate wrist pushes an errant strand of cocoa hair from her steam-filled dark eyes. She straightens up, resecures it in her Lucy poodle-updo, and tugs the bow of the organdy apron tied round her slim waist. Dad's home for dinner.

In fact, he's smiling a few feet away, shaking the silver bullet, and pouring their first nightly round of martinis on olives and ice.

He still looks good at thirty-nine, though strain is stamped around his eyes. It has taken months to recover from last year's heart attack.

But he's back at work now, writing and delivering two radio broadcasts a day. He can stand proudly at the head of the dining room table.

Before him, like symbols in a saint painting: a stack of plates, a steaming pot roast, and ravenous young faces.

"Betty, you found the carving fork!"

"St. Anthony suggested looking behind the stove and there it was," says Mom, sipping from her icy glass.

"Who's Sainanthony?" asks Skip. His booster seat is Webster's Unabridged, as it was and will be for us all.

"The patron saint of lost objects. We pray to him when we lose something and he helps us find it."

Crish, crish. Dad hones the long knife on a steel, slices and plates the fragrant gelatinous meat. Each plate passes from hand to hand to Mom for noodles, salad, and green beans.

Pogo, dark and darting king of imps, nimble of body and mind, pinches a nibble as the last plate goes by. He, too, is nearly recovered. He fractured his skull in the fall of that cardiac year and had to lay low for six weeks.

"Pogo! We haven't said Grace!"

"Grace is Gramma's name," offers Tom, ever aware of relationships. He's as blond as Pogo is dark, as conscientious as Pogo is spontaneous.

"But, Mommo, it's Grrrreaat!" roars Pogo.

"No commercials at the table. And please don't eat with your fingers. Where are your manners?"

"Ask Saint Anthony," Mary Kay quips.

Dad leads the Sign of the Cross: "*In the name of the Father, the Son, and the Holy Ghost. Amen.*"

Then Grace before Meals: "*Bless us oh Lord and these Thy gifts which we are about to receive, from Thy bounty through Christ our Lord. Amen.*"

The instant it's over, the cutlery clatters.

"Mary Kay, please change your fork to your right hand and put your knife down before you take a bite." Mom is on the job. "Don't slurp, Pogo. Please."

"How was the birthday party, Tom?" asks Dad.

"The sleigh ride was great—"

"Dad, is it a sin to kill a man if he pays you to do it?"

"Pogo, please don't interrupt."

"Like I said—"

"*As* I said, Tom."

"*You* just interrupted!"

"That's enough, Pogo," Dad warns. "What were you saying, Tom?"

"I got pushed off five times, but I got hot revenge!"

"He spit on me! Ick!"

"He didn't mean to, Mary Kay. Tom, please don't talk with your mouth full."

"Home, home on the Range," Skip is singing, skiing his beef through his noodles.

"Please, no singing at the table, Skipper, and no playing with your food."

"Irene's blobbing everywhere."

"She's a baby. You're a big boy now. You dressed yourself today, remember?"

"Pogo, elbows off the table, please."

"Can I have some more milk?"

"You *may* get it yourself. Tom, if you want the salt, ask your brother politely. No boardinghouse reach."

"He was hogging it." A punch to the arm.

"Ow! Quit it!"

"Boys!" Mom is frazzling. "What did you all do in school today?"

"Get me some milk, too, Pogo."

"Please," Mom suggests.

"Me too, please," says Mary Kay.

"No fair! Get your own!"

"We saw two movies, one about teeth and one on how to catch a cold."

"So is it a sin, Dad?"

"Words draw pictures," Mom says. "A sin to catch a cold?"

"Crimes are sins," says Mary Kay. "We had The Chief of Crime Prevention today. Did you know there are thirty-three crimes every day in Minneapolis? But he said television means more people are staying home, so not so many break-ins."

"Kracked-head Barrel, I was talking!"

"Pogo! Don't call your sister that!"

"She doesn't care, do you, Kakes?"

"You cracked your head, not I."

"Mary Kay, please don't bite your nails. You want to win the contest, don't you? Tom might be gaining on you. How are yours growing, son?"

"But Dad, is it a sin?"

Mom is exasperated. "These manners are atrocious. We can't even have a conversation. We have to do something."

Inspired, Dad sets down his martini glass.

"From now on, whoever makes a mistake in manners has to get milk for everyone else."

"Forever?"

"Until someone else makes a mistake."

Everyone agrees.

•••

But there are so many mistakes, the job keeps changing hands and it's hard to keep track. A few nights later, Pogo snatches the red paper cap from the milk bottle and offers a suggestion.

"If we crown the Milkman, we'll remember who it is every time! I wrote a song for us."

He sings (to the tune of "Sailing, Sailing, Over the Bounding Main"):

> *"Long live the Milkman,*
> *Long may he reign!*
> *For he's a schmo and we all know*
> *He's the gamest in the game!"*

From then on, the paper cap is placed atop the offender's head, the song sung lustily by all, milk refilled as needed by the offender. Seven rambunctious buckaroos learned table manners by means of ceremony, whimsy, song, and sharp-eyed siblings longing to relinquish the crown.

Within These Walls

The dining room door swings into the fierce emotional arena of the kitchen. If ever a room embodied conflict, this is it. What pleasures it holds. The bulging promise of Saturday's grocery bags, the body-swaddling aroma of a rich Sunday roast, the toothpick frills and sparkle of a black-olive party night—Ritz crackers, pimento cheese, Swedish meatballs bubbling in sauce; the humble rapture of just-baked cookies.

Yet what glaring, cold, hard surfaces. What unappetizing colors: metal-edged red Formica countertops, gray plastic wall tiles, an oval black enamel table, scrape-y chrome chairs, strange blue-gray-might-have-once-been-white striated linoleum, lit by an irritating flickering bare fluorescent halo. And, like the rest of the house, none too clean.

I see buttery, flowery, cozy kitchens at neighbors' or in magazines. "Mom, why does our kitchen look this way?" I ask over and over.

"It looked chic once," she answers. Throughout our childhood, she insists that she longs to redo it, but she never gets around to it. Truth is, it accurately reflects her loathing of domestic chores. Unless she's getting ready for a party, she dislikes spending time here. She states with pride that her favorite cookbook is Peg Bracken's *I Hate To Cook*.

While these dingy cupboards, counters, and fridge hold food, my principal source of comfort and happiness, these hard edges sharpen the stinky-sponged meanness of dishwashing arguments, tribal struggle, pilfering, and the delayed detonation of guilt.

•••

But come on, let's visit my living room.

We don't use this fireplace. Too much trouble since that time the flue wasn't open. The third and final time we lit a fire in it was to burn the mortgage.

These Meerschaums belong to Dad's whopping pipe collection. He loves a fragrant bowl of Brush Creek ever since he gave up cigarettes after his heart attack. What did break his heart?

Right there is our grandmother clock. It used to *bong* so beautifully, but hasn't worked in years. Just stuck there at 2:50.

This portrait hanging over the mantel is a jumbo of those Dad signs at the State Fair or down at the station. People line up to see Don O'Brien. He went from broadcasting minor league baseball games in his rich and resonant voice to radio programs, and now he's on TV.

•••

My father's voice is who my father is. Images, vivid and faded, advance and retreat on a screen in the mind, but voices enter the body like scent. I still feel your gentle resonance humming my shoulder against your chest.

The sound of you, the many pipe sounds: cleaning the stem with prickly pipe cleaners (Dill's, lettered red on yellow), knocking the bowl with the heel of your hand, the puff and toot, the skritching match, the suck of breath, your smoke-covered voice answering my questions, clink of the gone-out pipe against the grape glass ashtray.

He's sitting in this living room portrait, pipe in hand, as if paused in thoughtful conversation, more Walter Cronkite now than Gable.

Whether he's forecasting a good fishing day or buckets of snow on his evening weather segment, describing the comfort and durability of a King Koil Mattress, or hosting the Gold Award Theatre, people trust my Dad. For good reason.

He can say, "Go First Class...Go Phillips 66!" with real assurance, because he makes a point of always using the products he pitches. We go out of our way to get to Montgomery Ward.

Not only that, he screens the Hollywood Family Playhouse films before they air to see if they're worth watching. If not, he'll say, "It's a dog. Go to bed." The station goes along with what he calls his "frankness."

"If people are going to believe in the commercials I give," he tells them, "then I'd better be honest about the movies." It makes people want to shake his hand.

Integrity is his hallmark. He takes pride in that.

And see? His eyes really do follow you all over the room. Can't get away with anything in here.

Here's his gold reading chair, where once to amuse us he stood on his head. Here's where you'd find his lap if you needed it. Here's where I face the consequence of my first sin, at age five.

•••

It begins, as so much does, in the kitchen and centers, as so much does, on food.

"Can I have an apple, Mom?"

She's checking meatloaf in the oven.

"You mean, 'May I please have an apple?' "

"May I please have an apple?"

"You may not. It's too close to dinner."

I watch. When she turns to unscrew the jar of pimento-stuffed martini olives, I shove a Red Delicious under my striped polo shirt.

"Irene Marie! Did you just take an apple?"

"No," I reply bald-facedly, sure as an ostrich that I am concealed.

She folds her arms and scowls.

"Go speak to your father about this."

Stocking feet stretched on the footstool, he's relaxing in his gold chair reading the Minneapolis Star, tapping his index finger at intervals down the page.

"What are you doing, Daddy?"

"They're called obituaries, Honey. Listings of people who've died. I like to say a little prayer for each soul. What's on your mind?"

My heart slams my shirt.

"Mom says I took an apple when I wasn't supposed to."

"Did you?" he asks evenly, his eyes avoiding the fruit-shaped bump.

"No, Daddy." I gesture my innocence. On cue the apple drops to the floor, *bump, bump, bump* and rolls to his feet.

His face goes dark as Lent.

"Young lady, come here." In one swift movement, he yanks down my jeans, puts me over his knee, swats me once on the bottom, pulls my jeans back up and sets me back on quaking feet. It is the only time he ever does so.

"That was wrong. You disobeyed your mother *and* you lied about it. Take this back to her and apologize. Don't ever try anything like that again."

I am flabbergasted, horrified, ashamed. Daddy's never been mad at me before. Cast out of Eden, by an apple no less. But you just don't lie to Mr. Integrity.

•••

Beyond our long unfriendly davenport, upholstered in a nubby puce child-repellent fabric, bookcases teem with Churchill's World War II books, *Mein Kampf,* Civil War books, Steinbeck, Fulton J. Sheen, Conan Doyle, Poe, Hemingway, Chesterton, fat and varied Michener volumes, and *Books of the Month.*

Further random titles include *A Tree Grows in Brooklyn, Call It Sleep, My Name Is Asher Lev, Please Don't Eat the Daisies, Blackboard Jungle,* and *Pardon My Blooper.* This book screams us with laughter: "Ladies and Gentlemen, President Hoobert Heever!" "The fog is as thick as sea poop!"

Our low polished-slab wooden coffee table makes the perfect Steeplechase horse jump for me early Sunday mornings when everyone's asleep. *Look, Life,* and *Saturday Evening Post* are scattered on it now, along with Erector Set instructions, phonics sheets, somebody's speller, a couple Scrooge McDuck comics, Perry Mason's *The Case of the Velvet Claws,* and the butt-filled red plaid beanbag ashtray.

While Mom has a taste for serious lit—Dickinson, Byron, Shelly, Millay, Phyllis McGinley—she loves a nap and a paperback. Her trip to Rexall Drugs is not complete until the cashier rings up a couple mysteries with the Pepsodent. Josephine Tey, Mary Renault, Dorothy L. Sayers, Agatha Christie—she goes through them like we go through milk. Neither a driver nor a walker, Mom escapes family chaos in books.

St. Thomas More, patron saint of lawyers, presides over the carved desk. Dad graduated law school, but practiced only a short time before getting into broadcasting. Luckily, St. Thomas is also patron saint of large families.

And here's our aquarium of angelfish, black mollies, and guppies, which only Dad can feed them. I mean it.

The screened porch out back is the best place to be in a storm—not out or in. Smell the greeny rain, feel its mist spray softly through the screen, quake unharmed in the body-rumbling thunder. Maybe you're on Dad's lap in the wicker rocker, and he's telling you the story of Candyland, where trees and flowers are made of licorice and gumdrops and chocolate. In fall our porch is our turkey refrigerator. Twenty-two pounds.

•••

Let's go up my flying stairs. I'll save the sunroom for last.

Three stairs at the bottom, then a landing. Off to one side above the telephone table is a funny little hole in the wall whose origin we never knew. It is the exact diameter of a cigarette, and one day someone pops in a Pall Mall. Shortly thereafter, Tom sketches a simple face around the cigarette. This ballpoint fresco stays for years, with various augmentations—a mustache, a few penciled phone numbers. Ours is that kind of house. Neglect might induce creativity. A good joke stays put.

Up the remaining steps, past the door to the teeny balcony where Ro stuck her knee between the rails and firemen came and sawed her free.

Like everything else in our house, sleeping arrangements seemed to shift constantly. How do seven children grow up in a four-bedroom house? Sequentially.

The Littles regularly move in and out of this tiny daisy-flecked bedroom. Early on, that's where I slept, or tried to, in a bunk bed upper berth while brother Skip in the lower routinely kicked my mattress. When he moves to the big boys' room, Ro and I share. When I move, it's Ro and Jim. Then just Ro.

•••

Now pass the clothes chute (once a plunger got stuck there).

Here's *my* room from Kako when she joined the convent. Me and my mom and Tom put new wallpaper of blue with pink flowers on. Wallpaper paste smells good like Cream Of Wheat.

In my room I like to be by myself. When my feelings get hurt, flop on bed and scream in pillow. When I am bad they send me here.

I'm proud of Kako to be a nun so kind and loving. She is good, which I wish I could be. I'm like a stick on the ground who wants to be a ruler on teacher's desk, but how?

Sometimes I stay overnight at the convent, which I hope rubs off on me. I thought I'd see nun hair at night but they wear nightcaps.

On my walls I put my saint, my pennants, my black paper shadow a State Fair man cut, shelf of statues of two colts grazing and Morgan horse, china lady of my birthstone and two china nuns playing baseball that I had three but dropped the catcher and she broke.

In my window seat I read Bookmobile books, which comes by our school on Wednesdays. Get *King of the Wind*, *Misty of Chincoteague*, *Black Beauty* and every book of horses I love so much. Tame them, ride them, care for them, they always love you. I read everything about and draw them. If I only had one horse I would be happy as a millionaire. Or even just more horse statues.

Kako left me these three dolls of foreign lands to look at but I don't. Dolls are boring. I would give them to Ro but she'd pull them apart. If you're a girl you're supposed to have dolls but what do they see in them? Why pretend they walk or run around or talk when you can? Go outside and do it yourself.

The other thing I like in here is make things: cards, pictures, or of Play-doh that smells so salty and good or paint paint-by-numbers though I hate numbers, or sentences I really like to make.

Making makes you happy. Better than Monopoly because at the end you have something to give away or keep. But that's not easy.

You can't get it right, only so you feel okay if you stop. Everything goes wrong. Glue spills or your hand wrecks the line. All you want to do is throw the whole thing out because you spent all this time and all you have is something ugly. Sometimes you feel so bad and mad you never want to make another thing. Stomp outside to play or read your book.

But nothing's interesting or your eyes can't keep on your sentence and then you know you want to get it right so try again. And sometimes it's pretty good.

Next is our bathroom, big enough to walk back and forth of it. Our shower never works, so there Mom hangs her nylons.

Over the tub are sticker penguins washing who smile at you when I take my bath. What I love of baths is: to have bubbles and to wait until the water is almost gone and slip and slide back and forth it feels so slick and good.

Also in the tub, play with submarine I sent away to Kellogg's for which just put baking soda in and it swims but took so long to come now I don't send away even for sea-monkeys.

The best of all is thick mirror of the medicine chest. Swing it open, put your eye on the edge and see a whole green city of skinny green bars with no end. If you have to stay home just come to the mirror and go way far into Infinity City.

The blue colonial wallpaper in Mom and Dad's bedroom is punctuated by crucifixes, saints, and the Sacred Heart. Over the glossy cherry bed, a laden bookshelf sports a fluorescent tube for bedtime reading. Smells of pipe tobacco, Coty face powder, and personal parental scents.

They, too, have a window seat, where the Infant of Prague resides off-season. We bring Him downstairs for special occasions. He has a whole set of vestments for the liturgical year in purple, green, and gold brocade. I love dressing Him. Later, our first portable television finds a spot there. Reverberating here still is the gushy joy I felt when Mom invited me up to watch *An Affair To Remember* with her.

A triple mirror sits atop Mom's vanity table, which features a gold-doored triptych of the Blessed Mother, as well as *Cherries in the Snow* lipstick, tiny gold safety pins, drawers for cosmetics, lacy slips, and prosaic underwear. Red slidey tray of mascara which she can't apply without tearing up, so she stops. An atomizer with a fleshy tasseled bulb. *Evening in Paris, White Shoulders. Chanel No. 5* is her favorite.

Dad's chest of drawers is covered with bent pipe cleaners, handkerchiefs, coins, and Clorets. What coins pass through his hands, he examines. The best he keeps, inserted into blue numismatic books.

•••

They're gone. Look in their closets, Dad's of suits and shirts and wood egg things to go in shoes and Mom's of dresses and dusters and pedal pushers, poinky shoes and puffy party dresses. Right here I played doctor with David H. but lucky they never found out. Up top in a round plastic box: two velvet hats and collar of foxes with feet, eyes, and teeth who are biting each other's tails in a row.

When I go in their closets, it's like they are there.

With twin bunk beds and a single, the boys' room sleeps three brothers at any given time—first Pogo and Tom and Skip, then Tom, Skip, and Jim when Pogo leaves. A constant complex of smells— brass polish, shoe polish, sweet-smelling Butch Wax, Brylcreem and adolescence. All my brothers attended high school at a military academy and the required paraphernalia—clips and brass bits and hats and uniform sashes—spills from the room. Here's the fold-down desk Tom built to map and shelter the family genealogy on which he labors. Saggy chenille bedspreads, but topnotch uniforms, clean shirts, the cleanest in the house but for Dad's immaculate blue shirts—blue because he couldn't wear white on camera.

Behind this glass-knobbed door, a set of stairs leads to the desiccated, suffocating air of the attic—cardboard boxes, bins, outgrown moth-eaten whatevers, troves of old letters, a tatted blouse or two belonging to a grandmother. Place of discomfort and mystery—only utter summer boredom drives us up there, usually on solo expeditions.

•••

Oh, and the first floor sunroom? This glassy front room, ornamented with a few bony African violets from the last church bazaar, is lined with yet more bookcases holding Maryknoll *Crusade* magazines, atlases, a trim set of *Britannica,* and a ten-volume set of *The Book of Knowledge* (Great Saturday afternoon fodder. Did you know the Pyramids were so old they were in black and white?) We watch TV here, too, but that's not why we're here now.

This room compasses more of Mom's creativity than any other— she sewed these green slipcovers, made these muslin café curtains with Greek-key trim, and braided this huge rag-rug on winter nights watching Dad's Gold Award Theatre.

But best of all, on particular afternoons she lifts the center handle on this prosaic oak desk. A hidden hinge squeaks, a hidden spring twangs, a rough cough of metal. A whoosh of steely, oily, inky odor, and out of thin air, it appears.

Nothing in our house matches the theatricality of the typewriter ascending though its trapdoor in the desk, or the satisfaction of its *thunk* as it lands squarely in place every time, ready for action.

I love when Mom gets a phone call just as she's about to type, and I'm alone with the olive green L.C. Smith Secretariat. How pleasing to caress its toothy keys and fondle the silver oval on the carriage return.

Even more compelling, the orderly crescent rib cage of typebars, alluring to me as ship's hull to sailor. Keys are mere pictures of letters. Here's where they actually live. I love stroking that intimate arc, then pressing a letter into my fingertip, just to see. Wanting to press them all into my hands. Nudging a cluster of keys simultaneously to watch the bars rise and catch each other, releasing them back to their personal places.

My mother feeds this sturdy friendly animal fat sandwiches of onionskin and carbon paper and thereon types *"The Family Journal,"* a one-page newsletter of The O'Brien Household as dictated by her children.

Whatever else my mother could or could not give, she gives me this symphonic experience of writing, a big production marked with clacketing keys and the thrilling ding! of the carriage return. A returning carriage. Which carried words. Which are important. Which are important to write down. Which are important to share.

It doesn't happen often. But it happens. It almost makes up for not flying.

Montana, Day One:
Tenting Tonight

After setting up camp we all drive a half-hour to the little town of Seely Lake, where we gobble down decent pizza.

"How will Mom know we're alright in the wilderness?" asks Derek, Don's ten-year-old, a sunny buzz-cut towhead boy, even-tempered, slim. Leopard to his sister Lauren's lioness.

"Show him the GPS, will ya Mike?" asks Don.

"Sure," says Mike, pulling it from his pocket. "Once a day, I'll perch this doohickey on an open spot. The satellite'll beam 'We're OK' to Jolyne. Then she'll email your Mom and everyone's spouse. It can also say 'Send Help' if we need it and show our coordinates."

Satisfied, Derek folds in another slice.

•••

Later on, Jim and Ro and I stop at a bar overlooking the lake and share a sunset drink on the deck. They know I've been working on a family memoir. I confess my trepidation. "I don't want the people I love most to stop speaking to me," I tell them. "I don't want to hurt anyone's feelings."

"You can't worry about that," says Ro. "Write what you have to write. People will understand."

"Write whatever you need to," says Jim. "If my life can help somebody else, I'll be happy."

Hearing this from the two of them, even my DNA relaxes.

•••

The stars are just beginning to appear when we get back to camp. Mike drives the trailer over to the outfitters so they can pack the mules first thing.

Mike, thirty-five, Jim's eldest, is a law clerk and the "Ramrod" on our journey. He chose the route, rented two twelve-foot rafts, planned and procured six days' worth of food and supplies for the nine of us. Hired the outfitters, rented our horses and guide. He'll make all major decisions on land and water. Mike is also chief cook. Like his dad and brothers, this he relishes.

Although seven months pregnant with their baby daughter, his wife Jolyne has agreed to stay home and play single mom to year-old Creighton this week. This brainy, cuddly redhead knows the annual trip to the backcountry is lifeblood to these men.

Mike loves freedom. It's why he loves Montana: "They're not gonna tell you what to do. You don't wear helmets on horseback here. They figure you got common sense." His ideal trip would be off by himself in the backcountry on a horse with a dog at his side, but he'll go with us for this trip, his twenty-ninth.

Jack has been nearly as often. He's the chortling uncle you've always wanted, ever-willing to play games, and the first friend you'd turn to in crisis for counsel wise beyond his years. He's gotten time off at the taco shop—a job he likes since it gives him plenty of time to read philosophy and ruminate. He also enjoys dealing with the public. He can bike to work, the food's good, and it's locally owned, all of which deeply matters to him.

While Mike's at the outfitters, Jack and Don build a handsome campfire. A computer and marketing whiz for AAA, Don loves gadgets, technology, and camping with his kids. This, however, will be the longest camping trip he and Lauren and Derek have taken, but he seems prepared for anything.

Ro and I marvel at this skill set. Growing up in our house, we were lucky to get the plaid tin cooler packed with baloney sandwiches for our trips up to the lake.

We lean back in smoke-and-sooty spider-foldy steel-and-poly camp chairs. Jim slots red Solos into our cupholders, cracks a well-chosen single malt, and passes the bottle. We heave a communal sigh. We're here. It's begun.

A bouncing lance of light crests the hill. Mike's back. He pours a couple fingers in a red Solo, swigs, and says, "We spend tomorrow in camp."

"What happened?"

"Outfitters said too many in our party canceled." Some of Jim's friends and in-laws decided at the last minute not to come. "Had to give another group our horses. We go day after tomorrow."

We sit and sip. Immediate relief we're not riding at dawn. Only postpones the inevitable, though. How will I do? How will I hold up?

"Well, I'm gonna wash up. Where are the towels, Jim?"

"Hand it to her, will ya Jack?"

He offers a hand towel.

I laugh. "Joker. Could I have a bigger one, please?"

"That's it. That's our towel."

"You're kidding, right?"

"No. We keep it simple. Just the one."

"For *nine* of us? For *six* days?"

"It's all we ever use."

"Why didn't you let me bring my towel?"

"I honestly didn't think you'd need it."

He's serious.

"Jim, I need a towel."

"Okay, Mike—when you head into Seely Lake tomorrow, pick one up, will ya?"

"Sure."

"Thanks, Jim. Thought I'd have to pull the gauze out of the first aid kit."

"Oh, we don't bother with that."

"No first aid kit?"

"Naw. Few Band-Aids are enough."

Ro and I are dumbfounded. We shore don' wanna be quiverin' womenfolk burdenin' them saddlebags, but since when is safety sissy?

"Jim, this is wilderness! Mike, for us greenhorns, please get a first aid kit tomorrow."

"Oh, all right."

They are so casual. They are not trying to impress us with their macho. They all had to impress Grandpa Bill years ago. Now it's just how they travel.

It's good Ro and I have Big Agnes. We change into our pajamas and whisper our shared astonishment. The ground's lumpy, but the stars are beautiful. I want to leave open the mesh panels to look all night, but Ro is more experienced.

"If our sleeping bags get wet, they won't keep us warm."

She's no good when she's cold. I'm no good when I'm hot. We zip up and into sleep.

The Family Journal

That scuffed-up, cattywonkus house by the winding wild of Minnehaha Creek is physical bedrock to our family landscape. It's the only home Jim and Ro and I ever know. Even Mom and Dad have never lived so long in one place.

Before they landed in Minnesota, Dad's work as a sportscaster had led them round the Midwest: Omaha to Kansas City, Tulsa, Des Moines, and Sioux City. Each of The Olders was born in a different city.

By the late '40s, Dad was such a successful radio personality he was offered a job in New York, sportscasting for a major network. After talking it over, he and Mom concluded that New York was not a good place to rear children. (She was pregnant yet again, this time with me.) Instead, he took a new job as DJ at WDGY in Minneapolis. They liked the City of Lakes, and he'd no longer have to follow teams on the road.

One night in December 1951, shortly after moving house, Mom feels familiar contractions. Dad knows the signs of labor, but not Minneapolis. He puts Kako in charge, helps Mom down the icy sidewalk to the car, hops in, guns the engine and speeds down Nicollet Avenue, deliberately running red lights until a patrol car pulls him over.

"My wife," says Dad. "How do I get to the hospital?"

"Follow me." Cherry-top spinning and siren wailing, he escorts us to the hospital. I arrive safe and sound, with a bit of fanfare.

After four boys, everyone is glad for another girl. Mom especially. They name me after her beloved aunt. But newborn joy is snuffed by the shock of Dad's heart attack a few weeks later.

Mom can't drive, nor has she friends in this new city. For weeks, she's forced to take the Nicollet Avenue streetcar to visit Dad in the hospital. She's gone several hours each day, and what a frigid hell she must suffer, waiting alone in subzero air at the shelterless stop, aching with postpartum soreness, exhaustion, and hormones and icy with fear for her husband's life. Tears freeze in Minnesota even when they never leave your eyes.

That means Kako, thirteen, has to make meals, clean the house, get Pogo and Tom off to school, and tend two-year-old Skip and infant me. Much of my early care, then, is in the hands of my sister and brothers.

Dad's physical heart slowly recovers, but at this time, post-coronary protocol means abstinence from any kind of exertion and exercise. Dad had been a sportsman—a swimming and diving champ. Though he takes up fishing and swaps cigarettes for a pipe, his broken heart never recovers from that loss of vigorous physicality. It must be hard to have a houseful of children pulling on him, wanting to play, hard to tell them he can't wrestle, can't even toss a ball.

(Well, not *every* kind of exertion; within a year Mom's pregnant again.)

Just as Dad gets well, Pogo fractures his skull playing football. During his long convalescence and absence from school, Mom devises ways to keep this bright boy engaged and entertained. Chief among them, *The Family Journal.*

•••

Mom has made up a bed on the sunroom couch for Pogo so she can keep an eye on him. Because of his head injury, he's barely supposed to move at all. She comes in with her afternoon cup of coffee and a pack of cigarettes.

"How are you feeling, son?"

Silence. He's buried in a book.

"What are you reading, dear?"

"Count of Monte Cristo."

"It's a good book, but you've been reading for hours."

"Yeah, well, it's good."

"I'm going to write a letter to our relatives and let them know how well you and your father are doing."

She pulls the typewriter up out of its foldaway haven in the desk.

"Typing? Now? Can't you just write?"

"I have to make copies, son. Carbon is the only way."

"Please, Mom, I'm reading!"

I like to think a ray of golden late-day sun beamed onto the desk just then.

"How would you like to be the Editor of a Newspaper?"

"What do you mean?"

"Instead of me writing a letter, let's do a newspaper. You be the Editor and dictate stories. I'll be the Printer and type them up and send them to everyone."

"Hot dog!" We all want our names in print.

"But you have to stay still, son. Doctor's orders."

So begins *The Family Journal*, a fetching little freshet in our landscape.

The first issue is dated December 4, 1952.

Designated both "Editor" and "Reporter," Pogo dictates short items while "The Printer" types them onto onionskin, complete with masthead, headline, and columns, making ten carbon copies in the process. Every night, the one-page original appears on Dad's dinner plate; every week, the carbons are mailed to out-of-town relatives.

It's published intermittently through 1955—sometimes there's a new issue every weekday; then none for several weeks.

The one hundred or so issues in the morgue are a sweet, funny, and intimate record of one lively mid-century American household as told by its children.

News items range from awards and school plays to blizzards, colds, earaches, and the occasional original verse. Here we see family rituals, budding personalities, kid humor, and how we entertained ourselves in the early fifties. Our family with our "Waltons" faces on.

It's where "Kracked Barrel Head," "33 crimes in Minneapolis," "the lost carving fork," and the lyrics to the Milkman song are found (as if I could ever forget them).

The emphasis on manners threads from repeated rotations of The Milkman's Job through our behavior in public at the rare event of a restaurant dinner (both Mom and Dad write how proud they were of the family) and the creation of:

"POLITENESS DAY—everyone treats his brother or sister not as a brother or sister, but as a person! A great success."

The pages are a salmagundi of Bishop Sheen, Andy Griffith, and Art Linkletter, noting Saint's Days and altar boy practice, classroom achievements, humorous anecdotes, out-of-town visitors.

Charitable works: sewing pads for cancer patients, making scrapbooks for hospitalized children.

Building a beautiful snow fort. Birdwatching. Butterfly hunting ("Caught one, but let it go.") Stamp-collecting. Listening for distant radio stations. Playing Scrabble and Clue ("The new rage in the O'Brien household!") Exploring the new paint-by-number sets. ("Looks just like a real painting!" Even Dad does one or two.) Scanning the neighborhood with binoculars, spotting a turtle, capturing it, identifying it (according to *The Book of Knowledge*, a Snapping Turtle), keeping it as a pet awhile before releasing it.

WANT ADS:

"Wanted—person to do fifth-grade homework at low fee. Must be very honorable. Ask for Tommy."

"For Sale: snow shovel. Cheap. Please do not notify Dad of this sale. Contact the boys."

Next day: "Retraction: snow shovel not for sale. Dad read the paper."

"Wanted: Cleaner boys. For sale: grimy boys."

"Anyone who has not read Tommy's magic book is requested to refrain from doing so. He needs an audience and it isn't much fun to do tricks before people who already know about them."

Three-year-old Skip wants a tricycle license, so Mom issues one:

"Skipper O'Brien is licensed to operate a 1952 tricycle, signed President of the Department of three-wheeled vehicles in the O'Brien household."

In addition to Pogo and Dad on the mend, the paper reveals that someone is always sick: a cold, an earache, or the flu. And one kid or another is always saying The Darndest Thing.

Skip: "That's so funny it makes my nose laugh."

Kako writes about three-year-old me:

"When I asked her what her upper lip was, she informed me that was where she put her mouth. When I asked what her shoulder was she told me that was where she put her arm. When I asked her what her ankle was she said it was 'where I put my sock on.' "

You get a sense of the intellectual and moral issues posed at our dinner table. Here's the resolution of the earlier debate:

Dec 31, 1952

"We had a good discussion last night on whether it was a sin to kill a man if he paid you to do it. We reached the conclusion that the only time you can kill is in self-defense. It was a very interesting discussion ranging from the last war to the martyrs."

One night, a practical exploration of the legal process:

Jan 13, 1953

O'Briens Hold Court Last Night; Pogo Found Guilty; Jury Deliberates Two Min.

"Pogo was tried and found guilty of the crime of calling Tom a fig. Judge Don O'Brien presided, and accusations of Badgering the Witness and Contempt of Court were rampant. A countersuit was planned by the defendant."

There are also sweetly mundane items. A trip to the drugstore on a summer day "for ice cream and reading material." The children get comics, Mary Kay buys a photography magazine, and Mom selects "a couple pocketbooks and a Bartlett's." (I love this about her and about the drugstore—Bartlett's Quotations among Band-Aids and cotton balls.)

Newsflash from Pogo:

> "While I was dictating the first story I was also eating an orange. I was about to take it apart to put it into sections, and I was doing so when it went off. A steady stream shot at me from about a foot. It hit me right in the forehead and it was one of the longest, most accurate streams of orange juice that ever hit me."

We all eventually have columns, and each is beautifully, unconsciously revealing. In the first Kako's Kolumn, she shyly tells us her column is short, "So she doesn't take up too much of the paper."

She'll often comment on me. To my surprise, I learn from these pages that Kako, not Mom, is my principle caregiver.

As Editor and Reporter, Pogo's humor and verbal dexterity are evident throughout.

Tom's Topix is rare, but his columns display two outstanding characteristics. First, he's highly motivated by rewards. He wins a jacket by selling the most newspaper subscriptions. Another time, he gets $5.00 for earning a better grade.

Second, he often voices the extreme desire we all share to excel:

"The play I am in is tomorrow. I am wearing a girl's coat in the part of Santa Claus and hope that I will do well."

"I hope and pray that I will do well."

"I hope and pray I do a good job.... If we change the bird's cage for thirty days, we get a dog."

•••

Catholic bits are woven in and out. Father Dudley stopping by to
bless the house. Dad going on retreat. Getting our throats blessed on St.
Blaise Day. (You kneel at the communion rail. The priest crosses a pair
of beeswax candles around your throat, saying, "May Almighty God,
at the intercession of St. Blaise, bishop and martyr, preserve you from
infections of the throat and from all other afflictions." Very important
in a broadcaster's household.) Patron Saints and pagan babies
peppered throughout.

The Journal notes that Dr. Richdorf pays a house call and says Pogo
can go back to school half-days. After two months of home-schooling
Pogo, Mom includes rare personal commentary. She clearly misses him:

"It was lonesome with Daddy taking the children to school and just
the three of us left." (Skip, me and her.)

•••

The ticking pendulum and golden chime of our grandmother clock
sounded throughout our early childhood. Its arrival is noted. Pogo tells
us that "It was bought off a covered wagon by the sellers' ancestors."

•••

You can feel Dad healing in these pages—by March he can broadcast
the fights, which he relishes, especially now that he can't exert himself.
And he proudly covers a Yankees game—he loves the major leagues.

And now there's more money—the following September, we read
that Kako can transfer from public high school to Holy Angels and
next year Pogo will be able to attend a Catholic military academy. Like
Dad, all the boys will have a Jesuit education—morally sound and
intellectually vigorous.

The Jesuits are sometimes called the Marines of Catholicism. As
all O'Briens learned to be, they are devotees of philosophical debate,
propagation of the faith, and the progress of the soul. Jesuits echo all
over James Joyce.

We girls receive good Catholic education, too, including collateral Jesuit training since Dad and the boys love to debate and practice on us.

When I learn about Wall Street, I ask my father, "Do we have any stock?"

"All our stock is in our children," he says.

They invested in *us*.

•••

In 1953, *The Family Journal* masthead includes: "Reader: Don O'Brien; Newsboy: Skipper; Society Editor: Irene. (Though I am but two years old, it surely tickled Aunt Irene, who had been Society Editor for the Omaha World Herald.)

Mom's voice turns up from time to time:

> "Printer's Note:
>
> The Editor is on the phone, the society editor is screaming in the printer's ear because it is too late to go outdoors, the TV set is on so loud I can't think—Pogo and Tom have been having a conversation with one at the head of the stairs and the other at the bottom—in other words, zero hour, and the noise is terrific. It will all subside in a little while. Tom is serving Stations at 7:15. MK has a baby-sitting job at 6:30, Daddy has a game tonight, and the Littles go to bed—and then it will be lonesome for Pogo and me."

"I have to stop being The Printer and turn into The Cook."

•••

Plump, motherly, warm Anna Hansen, an intermittent fixture of our childhood, is mentioned here. We're well-off enough to hire a cleaning woman. She also made us the best Swedish pancakes on earth—with crispy buttery edges. She'd whip up a batch for Tuesday lunch and leave extras for us to eat after school—cold, rolled up with a spoonful of sugar. Proust never ate anything better.

According to Anna, at eleven months, "Irene is a wonderful child to entertain herself the way she does."

Designs for a basement rumpus room are solicited. Plans for a root beer stand discussed. Parties are noted. Mom holds a meeting of Sacred Heart Alumnae:

> "By dint of hard labor on the part of every member of the family... MK made brownies and tiny tea cookies and we served twenty Ladies! ...The table looked very pretty with a centerpiece of white carnations and blue iris."

On such occasions Kako dressed me up:

> "I put a pinafore on Irene this afternoon and she has been calling herself Alice all afternoon and asking if anyone has seen her rabbit."

•••

Here's the surprise party thrown by the Olders for Mom and Dad's fifteenth anniversary, featuring balloons, favors, hats, and "ice cream with a bell in it" for dessert. Mother gives Dad a combination pencil-lighter. He gives her a Swedish crystal vase and fifteen roses. Our gifts to them: "Bing Crosby's *My Girl's an Irish Girl* and *Galway Bay*, playing cards, a magazine for Dad and a green pencil for Mom, a comb for Dad and a comb for Mom."

•••

There's a summer gap from July till early September, when Pogo enters eighth grade and becomes a Junior announcer (his father's footsteps). After a few issues, though, there's a whopping hiatus of nearly two years, during which Jim is born.

But in January 1955, the Editor and reporters pick right up again for what will be the last three months of the paper until I assume editorship in 1964.

With the various school uniforms, "The O'Brien household looks like a Pentagon." Kako's a junior, Pogo's a freshman cadet at the military academy, Tom's in seventh grade, Skip's in kindergarten, I'm watching "Ding-Dong School," and baby Jim is in "Goo School."

The basement rumpus room, begun two years earlier, is completed at last by the three Olders, who "decided to get the job done once and for all." It's great for ping-pong, "Done up brown with green and yellow paint."

> "Wanted: Sure-fire paint remover for basement floor. NOT the kind that requires elbow grease."
>
> "Wanted: some good words for poor Mary Kay who is being woefully beaten at Scrabble every night by her parents."
>
> "Wanted: someone to play with Tommy, who owns the game."
>
> "Wanted: someone to feed the cub reporter while Mom gets dinner."

Heard in the kitchen:

> As we were sitting in the kitchen eating breakfast prior to the last mad rush for school, in comes Irene clad only in a pair of panties. When Daddy asked why she was not more appropriately dressed, she replied: "But Daddy, I can't find my sock!"

•••

I can be heard not only echoing my brother Skip—

> "At prayers the other night, after Skipper said, 'God bless Skipper and make him a good boy,' Irene said, 'God bless Irene and make her a good girl.'"

—but asserting myself as well:

> Skipper: "I just finished Irene's soup. All that good food going to waste. God made food for man to eat."

> Irene: "God made food for Girl, too."

•••

On March 7, in an item about watching Peter Pan that night, we find this sweet reveal: "This is the show that Dad saw five times as a boy." (How wonderful his parents took him.) The next day:
Family Watches *Peter Pan*—'Renie Can't Fly:

> Seeing Mary Martin fly prompted Irene to say in a mournful tone: 'I never learned how to do that.' "

Proof that by the age of three, both technique and memory of my stairway flights had vanished.

Pogo is now distinguishing himself as an expert marksman, a strong swimmer ("I learned how to swim last summer in order to avoid being a social outcast in our group"), and a fine young writer ("I got a ninety-seven on my short story and he wrote 'I enjoyed it very much' on it. PS: Copies of Pogo's short-story furnished free on request.")

Tom is industriously refinishing the living room tables and soliciting enough orders for his paper route to win the jacket. One of the most dramatic Family Journal stories shows his gallantry, courage, ingenuity, and humility all at once:

"When I was coming down the hill from school, I heard some yelling by the creek. Naturally, when I hear screams, I follow the path of the noise. It seemed that a girl had dropped her books while on the bank of the creek, and at this time of year that is always covered with ice. The book slid onto the creek on a thin layer of ice. The girl, presumably her name was Joan, tried to get it and slipped in herself. Since she was heavier than the book, she went in up to her ankles. It was

so slippery she couldn't get out by herself. The other girls couldn't get
her out, either, so they screamed for help. I got there, and discovered the
situation, and you know the Irish, always willing to help. First, I grabbed
a tree and told the other girl to hold on to my other arm, she did so and
I pulled her out. She was crying. Then there was the problem of rescuing
her 45¢ book. Some of the girls said, 'Joannie's life is most important,
don't try to rescue the book—you may fall in too.' But I was willing to
try. On my way down the bank, I got a jumping rope from one of the
girls that I tied onto a tree and lowered myself down sensibly. I got the
book with a stick. Then they said 'Thanks a LOT, Tom' while they were
seeing that the book and Joan were OK. I sneaked away quietly."

•••

Kako notes that her Junior-Senior prom (she's a junior) is "tripping
up on cat feet," a month away.

> "Mother and Mary Kay are beautiful again, they hope, after
> their permanents. We spent all Sunday afternoon in curlers
> and we hope that the Lord understands. And when the frizz
> comes out, we should be fashion models!"

Mary Kay Gets Formal:

> "After an afternoon of looking and trying on many formals,
> Mom and MK came home with a BEAUTY! It's blue net with a
> dropped shoulder and tiny puffed sleeves... It has a lace bodice,
> and a full net skirt. Tiny pink roses are scattered on the skirt. I
> just love it and Irene said, 'Oh Kako, it looks so pretty. You look
> like Alice!' (Alice in Wonderland, Irene's highest compliment—
> if you look like Alice, you're in!) We also bought Irene a new
> Easter hat—white with pink flowers on it and ribbons down the
> back, and when we showed it to her she said, 'Oh mommie, I
> knew you would bring me a cowboy hat!'"

•••

Even I think it sounds like a riot to grow up in this family, like Cary Grant saying, "Everybody wants to be Cary Grant. Even *I* want to be Cary Grant."

But between the lines on those yellowed onionskin originals, unspoken fissures of anxiety emerge.

The last issue of the first run on March 29, 1955, informs us that the cabin at Prairie Lake in Northern Minnesota has been reserved. Up at the lake. Out in the woods. Lifelong gifts.

Montana, Day Two: Practice

We hang out in the woods by the lake next day, getting used to walking five minutes to the RV campground for water, still gratefully in restroom range, regularly eyeing that slice in the mountain, knowing pain and challenge, along with beauty, await on that trail in the morning.

While Mike goes into town, Jim offers me a fly fishing lesson. The guy just loves to fish. I remember him barely taller than the minnow bucket he fished in.

"Let's practice in the parking lot. It'll narrow your focus."

He's a clear and patient teacher.

"First pay out your line." He lays out twenty feet. "Here's the grip—thumb on top, in line with your forearm. Keep it steady. Now here's what you're after."

He demonstrates the swooping grace of the classic fly-cast. My heart lifts. Such fluid freedom, as though he flicks away arthritis through the dancing line.

He sets me up.

"Think of a clock arcing over you. Cast from ten to two. Ten-two, ten-two. Don't break your wrist—keep it steady."

I try the clockwork.

"Good. Feel it. Ten-two, ten-two. Better."

Hm. I might get this.

"Aim for that clump of leaves."

The idea of aiming freezes me. I want to be successful, but I really want Jim to feel successful as a teacher. What if I never catch on?

"You can do this. Just takes time. There you go."

Before long, I make three good casts.

"You've got it. You've got it!"

"I get it!"

"You're a natural!" We squeal and hop and hug each other. One of the best moments we've ever shared.

•••

That afternoon, Mike returns with a (hand) towel of my very own, a small first aid kit, and a mess of seafood.

"Can't eat it on the trail, but we can tonight." He hauls out the Papa Bear cast-iron cauldron and over the campfire concocts a rich, herby cioppinno. Lauren assists.

"I want to be a chef," she declares. "But a pastry chef."

As we fill our bowls, her dad rummages in his pack and produces a canister of "Slap Ya Mama" Cajun seasoning. Don thinks of everything. Cheers and subsequent slurps all around.

•••

After our steaming spicy bowls, another bottle of Scotch appears. Don stands and motions to Lauren.

"We have a present for you, Jim."

I smile. I have a present for him, too. A very special bottle. But not until our last night.

"Lauren and I invented this a few trips ago."

They lay a brand-new nylon tarp and Sharpies on the ground.

"It's a Story Tarp. Every day, we each draw a pictograph of our most memorable moment. Then the whole story goes home with Jim."

We all grab markers and scramble to record the day. I look up from drawing me fly-casting. Jim's drawing the same thing.

Then Ro says softly, "I've written a song for the trip. Wanna hear it?" (Curiously, from her earliest days, Ro's asked permission to sing.)

Of course we do. Firelight flickers over her notebook, gilds her gently knit brow. She sings a yearning ballad of "wild Montana," of her hope to shed her fear and sorrow here. Closest to our late brother, his death and absence weigh on her, but fear and sorrow have slipped, admittedly or not, into everyone's pack. Her last verse asks for laughter, "grand and holy." Shining eyes ring the campfire as her last note fades.

Soft applause, congratulations and gratitude ripple from us all.

"Gotta call it a night," says Mike at last. "We need to get up before dawn, break camp, wolf a bagel, and get to the outfitters."

Heartened by her song, we peel away to our downy nests under the stars.

Between the Lines

This *Family Journal* item is one tip-off that not all is well in Tangletown:

"The race between MK and Tommy is waxing hot and heavy. This battle is to see who can grow long nails." What's making these children anxious? Why are they biting their nails?

Skipper joins the contest, showing "strong will power." He is only three years old, and he is already chubby as well. What makes him so nervous at this tender age? It is he who wins the competition.

Kako and Tom continue the contest between the two of them; Tom wins. He spends the $5.00 prize on a new Missal and Valentines (which indicate the breadth of his values).

Why does Kako lose? The pages answer. Kako, not Mom, reads us bedtime stories. Kako is making doughnuts and cookies and raspberry pie, comforting us and herself with them. O'Brien stress goes into our mouths.

Kako is even buying my clothes: when I'm a year old, she brings home "sox, a shirt and a darling little plaid dress—blue top and a plaid skirt, on the pocket in red it says 'Me.' "

I wear it the next night when the family goes to a restaurant—a rare event, indeed. According to the paper I try "out-staring the ladies at the next table and won."

Kako, not Mom, takes note and proudly reports.

The most startling entry concerns a little brown bump of birthmark at the nape of my six-month-old neck. It lies smack in my hairline.

"Have it cauterized," the doctor advises. "Hairbrushing will aggravate it later on."

Dad drops us downtown at the Medical Arts Building, but it says here—surprise—Kako, not Mom, accompanies me to the procedure, then takes me home on the streetcar. Mom stays home to print the paper.

"You sure didn't like the elevator," they said when I was older. "You wailed all the way up to the twelfth floor and all the way down." Yeah, and I might have been wondering where my Mom was.

I still do.

And I am not the only one.

A Crystal Cave

Whole lotta shakin' goin' on in '56. Dad's radio station turns to a Top 40 format, and he wants out. WCCO-TV snaps him up as on-camera weatherman and movie host. (He also tries to create a children's show featuring himself as a friendly pirate, but no go.)

The Olders are now in high school. Tom's a freshman at the military academy, Pogo's a junior, and Kako graduates in June. The phone is either ringing or monopolized, and there's a flurry of shaving, corsages, and other dating accoutrements. Well, not so much for Kako. She has steadily gained weight and lost confidence.

For graduation, Mom and Dad buy her a suitcase and take her out to dinner. Just the three of them. The kicker comes over dessert.

"I've decided to become a nun. A Benedictine."

Clink go their coffee cups. They are openmouthed.

"Honey, you're too young," Dad insists.

"No I'm not. I turn eighteen in December, and I can enter then."

"I know it sounds exciting now, but please, honey, wait a year. You need to live a little."

"I've lived enough to know it's what I want, Dad." She is adamant. She wants to be out of the house and free of her undeserved duties of motherhood, but of course cannot state her true feelings. So she insists on her "vocation."

They are unable to sway her. This tenacity is the surprise in Kako's character. For all her apparent malleability and acquiescence, my sister is a mass of granite when she wants to be.

That summer is the last one she'll share with the family. We have a picnic and fly kites—the one and only time we ever do so, renowned in family lore as The Day We Flew The Kites, as if such exotic activities were only possible once.

That December she becomes a postulant at The Priory in St. Paul.

•••

Years later, after Kako's left the convent, we talk.

"When did you know it wasn't for you?"

"The first day. The nuns had assured us that postulants kept their hair, and then cut ours off the very first day. We felt so betrayed. We were prisoners. Even if we wanted to leave, we couldn't go back in the world with no hair."

"What about your vocation?"

"I never really had one. I was fat. Who would ever want me? That left two choices: teacher or nurse. I hated blood, and thought if I were going to teach, I might as well be a nun. So I stayed."

Within six months, unbeknownst to us, she's drinking heavily, and will for several years.

•••

Early in 1957, Mom finds she is pregnant yet again. Ro is born at the end of September. That year Jim, three, suffers a hernia and is hospitalized for the first time. I start first grade.

In 1958, Mom makes a New Year's resolution to "make carbons of the family activities, similar to what we used to do with the Journal"—a weekly update for relatives and another record of illuminating detail.

That April, Mom, Ro and I (age six) fly to Omaha so Aunt Irene and Uncle Harry can meet the baby. Here she addresses Aunt Irene about our departure from Omaha:

> "Do you remember how (Irene) looked when we got on the plane?...navy blue coat, her shiny patent leather 'party pumpers' and the white Easter hat with daisies all around the brim? She looked like an angel—fond mother talking—with her curls cascading down the back. Well, we got on the plane, fastened the seatbelts, and she turned to me and said "I'm tired of fighting with Skipper, but if he starts anything, I'll put up my dukes!' I just gasped—the visit was over and so were the elegant manners!!"

I clearly dread returning to my brother's bullying, but "fond mother" gasps at my manners. She wanted a dainty topiary to grace her wildboy park. Instead, I'm a mess of kudzu sprawling wild in all directions, useless to clip.

But Skip makes me so mad all the time because what did I ever do to him? He likes to hurt me: Paper Scissors Rock to lick his fingers and slap me hard on the wrist or pretend to be nice then whack my cheeks or put his arm around my shoulder all "Pal-sey Wal-sey," then trip me.

Why can't he be nice like little Jim who has no mean bones and whose jokes aren't funny, but so cute. Tries to help you, not jump to scare me, pound on top of me, Dutch Rub Wrist Burn try to make me wet my pants.

But Mom says if you can't say something nice about someone don't say it at all, so I won't.

Six months later:

"This will be a big week, for Saturday morning Irene makes her First Holy Communion. She can't wait...she is on a diet, now— overweight—and is being so careful about what she eats."

But my feelings can't be let out, so my beautiful Swiss-dot First Communion dress has to be.

•••

I start having terrible nightmares and can't fall asleep. Things I see on television are the ostensible cause—scary Jack-in-the-box Twilight Zone, Johnny Tremain spilling molten silver on his hand, a Bonanza where a guy's paralyzed—but no doubt I am responding to my local bogeyman brother and other inexpressible fears.

Dad, not Mom, is always the one who comes in to say it's all right.

"Where's your rosary?" he gently asks. Crammed in a drawer to hide its spooky green phosphorescence, but I can't tell him that. To read, he hands me a parish bulletin with plans for the new church; to sleep with, a picture of the Sacred Heart of Jesus.

•••

Church I pretty much like. Our house is always messy, even though Anna comes on Tuesday, which Mom makes us clean up before she comes, but church is always clean and peaceful, except when they remind us how bad we are, which is mostly all the time.

Oh I wish I were as good as Cinderella and be happy and quiet to do my work and dream but I get so mad.

My brothers get to rake and mow which who wouldn't rather have burning leaves or cut grass smell, warm sun like pancake syrup or cheeks tight shoveling clean snow, instead of skinny sad sunlight on davenport, the dust you dust dries up your nose or stupid vacuuming.

Outside, someone laughing running down the sidewalk, but kitchen scrub brush croaking like a broken locomotive over dirty gray linoleum, stinky water dirty, everything wet, won't suck back in sponge, stupid floor won't come clean.

After floor, sit with tired legs apart. Mom comes by, flops them together, "Be a lady quick!" Everyone says how cute Ro is how sweet Jim is how funny Pogo is how kind Tom is how holy Kako is how smart Skip is what about me? I turn into a tornado with blades of anger flying out, wanting to break a window in the sunroom, rumble the neighborhood down, getting madder screamier whirlier can't stop I'll explode. Mom throws cold water on me. I stop. I have to. To breathe.

Then sour hurty feeling. Devil's horns prick my conscience for doing bad, which you have to feel though it hurts because otherwise his horns wear down and you do bad all the time and don't feel it.

Jesus is the first I learned how bad we could get. Because Jesus is as good as we could get. He didn't do anything to them, only tell stories, do miracles, love everybody, and only got mad *once*, which why kill Him for that? Thorns in His head, heavy cross, nails in hands and feet, hanging bleeding dying, which why? He was the best man ever. Plus God.

Our sins crucify Him again and again.

Hard to sleep.

•••

The anxiety is not just mine. Pogo develops psoriasis. Skip is getting fatter. Jim continues to injure himself in ways large and small. Mom describes him asking for a Band-Aid for a scratch. She doesn't think he needs one, but he says, "Look, there's the blood charging out, now I need one."

By age four, Jim has bitten his nails to infection. The doctor finds them nearly gangrenous and Jim is promptly hospitalized again. He confides, "They say if I'm good, they'll let me keep my fingers."

•••

The truth isn't found in the carbons of her letters.

Nor is it dramatic in an ordinary way. We're not hit, there's food on the table. We even have fun.

But we're like the little monkeys with the wire mother. Mom's soft arms weren't for hugging, but for folding at her chest; her mouth not for kissing, but compressed in resignation—her chief expression in thirty years of snapshots. She could let life through her body, but not up against it. And all our bodies knew it.

The distance a mother keeps from the bodies of her children is the distance they will keep from their own.

I have seen her icy even with her own grandchildren, shudders sickening through her at their embraces and requests. I have seen her fidget with a baby on her lap as though he were a frozen tuna.

Mom sprang from her own thorny landscape: a lonely girl, longing for family, trained as the ladiest lady, all dainty napkins and luncheons, seashell soap, scalloped dishes, all that is breakable, linen, or white.

Her heart is a cave of crystal we come crashing through.

Children were her childhood dream but her waking nightmare— dirty, shitty, boisterous, sneezing, laughing screeching farting weeping swearing.

But no child knows this kind of thing. She simply knows, no matter what, that it's her fault.

•••

A mother's love: the fundamental promise of the animal kingdom. Every childhood emblem: robins in the nest, the nuzzling foal. Instinct powerful enough to lift a station wagon off a child.

Something made my mother flip the station wagon onto me. I must be flawed, I must make up for it: entertain, inspire, make proud. What if the baby robin pulled a rabbit out of the nest or the foal turned cartwheels over the field?

You are not of my species.

But I *am*. Just bind my wings with wire. Chain my hooves to a stake in the ground. See?

Except it hurts. Movement unimpeded is the first promise of the physical, preceding even motherhood.

Kick and scream all over the floor, lovely floor, welcoming sweet bams of fists and feet.

Which does not win her. But which wins relief.

Twinkles

Dad's back. I run to give him a hug.

"Dad...!"

I'm too big for him to swoop up but he leans down and hugs back.

"Hi, honey."

"Hi, Mom." She's just returned from a five-day visit with Aunt Irene and Uncle Harry. She's too dressed up to enter through the back door, but Dad parked in the garage.

"Irene, what did you do to your blouse?" she asks. "And why are you still in your school clothes?"

"My fountain pen leaked. And I was just gonna change."

"'Going to,' not 'gonna,' " my mother says, stripping off her thin kid gloves and heading for the front hall closet.

"How was the plane?" I want to know.

"Golly, it's wonderful to fly. I lit up a cigarette, read my *Redbook*, and I'm in Omaha."

Dad helps her with her coat. She removes the green pillbox from atop her deflating bouffant and sets it on the top shelf.

"Of course, then I lit a cigarette and read a *Family Circle* and I'm home."

"What did you bring me?"

"Irene Marie! That is very rude. And I didn't bring you anything. You're a big girl now."

"Our lady sitter likes us better than you. She reads to us and bought us Twinkles. In the storybook package."

"You know I don't believe in sugar cereals."

"But the box is a book! It's a story."

"Please go change your clothes. I don't know how I'm going to get that blouse clean. I wish you'd be more careful."

"Well, I wish you hadn't come back..." I surprise myself. It's true and it's terrible. A lava of confusion chases me upstairs.

After dinner, Dad draws me aside.

"You hurt your mother very much today."

I'm dumbfounded. I thought you could only hurt people who cared, I want to say, but I don't.

"I'm sure you didn't mean it. Tell her you're sorry."

But I did mean it. Dad wants me to lie? Confusing and terrible, too. Integrity notwithstanding, there are times when the truth should not be told.

Montana Day Three:
Angels on Horseback

"Morning. You guys awake?" Mike's flashlight sieves through an orange wing of Agnes.

"Yup."

Stretch a bit. Bumpy ground. Ro showed me the way to line up my stuff to make dressing in not-so-Big Agnes easier. We grab the West's idea of a bagel and break camp before day itself breaks.

When the cars are packed, it's off to the outfitters to saddle up.

Angels on Horseback. Where'd that come from? Mom. Fancy canapé—bacon-wrapped oysters. She loved a pretty phrase.

Pink glow strokes the string of waiting horses.

I don't want this day to start and I want it over with. Calm down, Irene. Look at Lauren.

Champing at the bit. She wants to jump on a horse, jump off a raft, jump into life.

I don't want to jump. I want to tolerate. Light-headedness? No breaks? Pain? A cup and a half of water for eight hours in summer sun? I'm no good in heat. Ask my husband about the day I flipped out at noon on a dune in Egypt.

Breathe deeply, Irene.

Jim holds out a handful of little blue pills, anti-inflammatories he uses for arthritis.

"If you want one, you're welcome to it."

Ro passes. "If there's a likelihood of light-headedness, I don't want to compromise my balance, or make myself more light-headed."

Not me. If today's going to be miserable, the more help the better. I swallow one.

All packed. Time to mount Sugar. At least she's not a huge, wide horse. But as I swing my leg over the saddle, my well-stretched inner thigh takes a terrible hitch. Oh no. Did I just dislocate it? Will it hurt the whole doggone rest of the trip? Relax.

I am out of every comfort zone but love.

•••

We begin the ascent up the fold of land we'd eyeballed for two days and find we are entering clemency.

This land is a governor's pardon. Instead of scary cliffs of scree, we're riding through immensely varied and beautiful terrain: dense moist forest followed by lyrical passages of wildflowers—fireweed, Indian Paintbrush, goldenrod. A broad field brimming with masses of creamy-plume beargrass. A delicate vale giving onto a creek quivering with thousands of burnished gold butterflies. Nabokov's dream.

I unwind into awareness. I am surrounded by family, nine of us again, people who know and love me, whom I know and love, who know what they're doing out here. Good to be around kids, too—Don's are so confident and happy with their bodies. He's so affectionate with them. With all of us.

Derek's spirited little mount Dolly delights in her light load: a wiry, eager ten-year-old boy. She comes clippiting past and pops in front of me, which prompts Sugar to trot. Bumpity bumpity, bouncing my bones. She won't slow. Oh, enjoy it, Irene. That riding class forty years ago— how do you post again? My thighs grip, remembering for me. But it's a rough ride.

None of the other horses catches the trot itch. What's going on?

"'Course she wants to keep up," Bud, our guide, explains. "Dolly's Sugar's mama."

I laugh. From now on, we keep a few more horses between me and Derek. Lauren's black mare won't cooperate. She tosses her head, pulls on the bit, won't respond to Lauren's direction, and halts whenever she pleases. Eventually Lauren hooks a rope up to Bud's horse so "I don't have to worry about steering."

Domenic is also having trouble managing his horse.

A bright, recalcitrant fourteen-year-old, Domenic is slim, strong, and thanks to trips with his Uncle Don, comfortable in all things REI. He has a command of technology, a fascination with engineering, and an interest in writing.

"I want to write something like *Hitchhikers Guide*."

He's already written a young adult novel, available on Amazon, which I read before I came. While he can sustain a narrative, he confesses he delayed proofreading until the night before it went on sale, leading to moments of unintended humor.

His horse is still misbehaving, but soon, contrary to Jim's prediction, Bud gives us and the horses a break. We slide down, stretch, pee, walk around.

A sparkling stream gushes nearby. Our mouths water for it, but Jim hadn't seen the need for a filter.

"Aw, I just drink from the river."

"Yeah, but Dad, you got Giardia the last couple times," says Jack.

"Yeah, well, that's how it goes."

Jim has an abundance of backwoods knowledge and a lack of common sense. In him it's oddly endearing.

Don to the rescue again. It's a fairy tale every time he reaches into his bag. He retrieves a portable water filter. In moments, we're sucking down cold mountain water, to the deep content of our animal natures.

I'm grateful I, too, have a boon to offer my companions: my chamois cream. Many takers.

Back on the horses. The day bends over the trail. We fall silent awhile.

Riding through a thick patch of greenery, Bud leans out from his horse and hacks off some leafy branches.

"Take one and pass 'em down."

Fresh huckleberries, stripped directly from their twigs with teeth and lips. Sweet bursting jewels.

We pass shimmering lakes, a hefty wedge of glacier, vivid young pines reclaiming burned land. It's a pleasure riding my responsive and agreeable horse over such scenic, well-maintained trails. My preparatory stretches, padded bike shorts, chamois cream, and the little blue pill are keeping me fairly comfortable. But it's now Hour Ten. Of our Eight-Hour ride.

We come to a juncture that calls for tough equestrian choreography. The horses must make a short, steep, rocky ascent, immediately and arrhythmically step over a large fallen tree, and then instantly pivot into a sharp rocky descent. Most make it smoothly, but Domenic's horse spooks, leaves the trail, and bolts for a standing dead pine. A branch catches the chin strap of Domenic's hat, tearing it off, but he keeps his seat and his wits, retrieves his hat, and guides the horse back onto the trail.

"You okay?"

"Yeah."

"Great job, Domenic!"

We proceed. I'm riding just ahead of Domenic when he says, "I think I'm bleeding."

"See if he's okay, will you, Irene?" Don calls.

I turn in my saddle and freeze. There, jutting three inches out of his left temple—"Domenic. You have a stick sticking out of your head."

Whereupon he screams and bursts into tears.

We halt. Don leaps down, helps him dismount and carefully extracts the sharp dart of wood.

We're all shaken, none more than Domenic, but once all seems well, Jim claps him on the back. "Now you have a story."

I love my brother so much for the gift he just gave that frightened kid.

Domenic blushes with pride.

I begin to understand what Jim seeks and finds out here.

Later in camp, Don cleans the puncture wound and the scalp scrape and applies antiseptic cream. Jim offers Domenic his first slug of Scotch. Which he hates.

"So Jim," I say, "aren't you glad we had the first aid kit?"

"Aw, we woulda just splashed whiskey on the wound."

I mark the event in my own way. I dig out my little kit and sew the chin strap back onto Domenic's river hat. With a stray bit of thread, I embroider a tiny red star inside the brim, just at the spot of his injury.

By day's end, a smiling Domenic had come up with his take: "I was in a sword fight with a horse, and I lost." Which, of course, he didn't.

•••

The campsite's a beaut. Right at the river's edge. The packers and their mules have come and gone, leaving our heaps of stuff.

Mike makes chili while we pop up Big Agnes and get settled.

Jim distributes hefty cans of bear spray, one for each of us. They are like miniature fire extinguishers, and for once, Jim gives instructions.

"When the bear's twenty feet away from you—though fifteen feet's better—spray's more effective—pull this plastic loop latch and spray this bad cloud at the bear. It'll obscure his sight of you and mess with his nose. "

"You hope," Jack chimes in. "I had a friend go to Bear School? They train you to react quickly if a bear attacks. They put a crash-test bear at the top of a slide, with you at the bottom. The bear was released and came flying down, proving again and again you'll never have enough time to use your bear spray."

"Aw, the river'll kill me before a bear gets the chance." Now I'm talking like a Montanan.

"If you go off to pee at night, be sure and take it with you. Speaking of which, here's the folding shovel. When you need to do your business, get away from camp and bury it. Shouldn't look like anyone was here."

A home-cooked meal, laughter, talk, and Scotch. A cool, moonless, bugless night, perfect for viewing the immense carpet of stars materializing above us. Thrilling intermittent starry darts and arcs remind us the Perseids are soon to come. A night of starstruck sleep. And a sense of peace we won't know again for many days.

Shifting Sands

By September of 1958, our landscape shifts again. Pogo joins the seminary. The day Kako is allowed to join us for a visit is the first day the whole family has ever been together. We celebrate Ro's first birthday.

•••

Pogo went to Nazareth Hall which I'm shocked does not have palm trees and sand like *Book of Knowledge* Nazareth. It is sad he has to go because Pogo has a very funny humor to rhyme things and make faces and jokes and I was Reen-Bean and he was Pogo-Bogo now just a hole at the dining room table. Also hard to sing Deck The Halls with Boston Charlie and Be Kind To Your Web-footed Friends because he has special harmony so a hole in the songs now too. And Family Journal.

But Tom is still here and not mean like Skip. He loves our family and made our family coat of arms and drew our family tree down through the ages.

He's also smart for fixing things and business. Last summer he made up a business to paint everybody in our neighborhood's address on their steps and got money. Now, Junior Achievement with first aid kits he sells. He makes a mint for presents for everyone and to take girls out. The best of Tom is this one time.

•••

"Wake up."

Tom shakes me in the dark.

"The watertower, remember?"

I jump into my jeans and shirt. In short moments we reach a cherished place: the Washburn Watertower.

A massive masterpiece of art-deco, circled by Oscar-looking men with swords who guard its water, it stands high on a hill over the green treetops, domed like an observatory, like a crown in the skyline, like the head of the Pope, surveying the surrounding homes under the wide flat sky.

(Under the swordsmen we would stand, under the very points of their swords, pretend that they would drop them on us, pretend there was a mad scientist inside who wanted to rule the world; something more valuable than water had to be behind the wide huge mysterious metal bank-vault door.)

At the foot of this frightening fascinating overwhelming presence indicated by my big brother's pointing finger—his arm, straight and strong as a fine white baseball bat, quivering ever so slightly under the weight of the dirty canvas bag smudged with ink and mudballs full of morning papers fresh and curling slightly in the dawn damp—is what he'd spotted yesterday, told me about last night, brought me here this morning to behold. Huddled by the watertower steps, like a small forgotten child's fur slipper, teeny ears thin and pink as little fingernails, twitchy nose quick as her heart, cotton-tail no bigger than a Q-tip top: a baby bunny, her button eye filmed with the shock of abandonment.

She is small and soft as a baby's shoe, trembling, mute with patience, as I under the massive weight of Church ways and family ways; and Tom noticed it, wandered off his route to look away at the vista, and yet looked down too, to find this small thing at his feet, trembling like his little sister who longed to soothe her own thittering heart.

Together we bring a shoebox and flannel pajama bottom, pluck some grass and dandelion for a little home. He lets me put her in among his ribby socks, among his polo shirts she would be safe.

How did my mother find her—was I soaking a rag in milk, and did she ask why? Was I so joyful that she read it in my face: I have a little charge to nurse, and I will show you just how loving's done, since you forgot.

Return it to the wild, she said, you cannot raise it here. Touch it and the mother will abandon it.

The following dawn, laying the little brown breathing fur by the concrete steps, I wonder, "Who touched *me*?"

Into the Spotlight

Dad is becoming a real television personality. It's strange and fun to see him on TV, a father shrunk to one foot high in black and white, a doll of a dad, little arms pointing out barometric pressure systems. Or to look from Dad in the room to the Dad on TV, a mysterious glee.

The public and the private man aren't much different. He never swings celebrity around. When asked, "Are you Don O'Brien?" he'll say, "I'm guilty." That's it.

We love visiting the station, seeing the station break cards, the secret blue chalk viewers couldn't see that marked the weather maps, watching the thrilling big black cameras swing round, walking on the newsroom set, shaking the hand of Clancy the Cop, Twinkies in our goody bag.

Every year the station videotapes our living Christmas card: "Merry Christmas from the O'Briens to the viewers," huge hot lights drying up our Christmas smiles. And every year, on New Year's Eve, Dad holds a TV party for his viewers, folks without parties to go to. He orders in champagne and canapes, buys balloons and hats to dress the set. In white tie and tails he leans toward the camera with a champagne flute and a paper plate of goodies, saying, "Have some, won't you, while we watch the next act of *The Bells of St. Mary's*." On New Year's Day we wake up to balloons and foily hats left on our bedposts.

Dad's moving up, and Mom likes it. He makes personal appearances at the Minnesota State Fair. He's asked to join the regional chapter of Variety Club, a show business charitable organization which built a children's heart hospital at the University of Minnesota. Shortly thereafter, he's asked to join their board. My father's voice is who my father is. An authority, of course.

And yet to amuse us he stood on his head. No photos show this impishness, the twinkle and the whisper that fatherhood brought out in him: whacking out "It's neat to beat your feet upon the Mississippi mud" on his suit pant thigh.

Our local TV Guide does a feature on him. Because Kako can't leave the convent, our family portrait on the cover has us all gazing at her high school graduation picture in Dad's hands. Our first view of Earth was described by these hands: the lemon orbiting the orange in the square brown fingers. What security. We knew from how he held them they would never fall.

Seeing Dad on TV and in TV Guide makes all TV seem truer, and movies, too, because Dad tells the truth. And Father Does Know Best. So Donna Reed seems true as Mom (but nicer). When we look at Kako, we see *Song of Bernadette* and *The Nun's Story*. None of us knows she feels imprisoned and betrayed, is seeing a therapist, and is taking anti-depressants.

Fatherland

Father, father, burning bright in the questions of the night. What is you and what is me? Which is the movies? What is TV?

Images, vivid and faded, advance and retreat.

Our family begins in your family—you born in 1913, reared, like Mom, in Omaha. It was not white-clapboard, but the heavy dark-stone, brown-brick weighty Midwest.

Not so many years before, Irish immigrants drawn by railroad jobs could find no housing here. They dug homes out of earth, on open plains just north of Omaha. Folks called it Gophertown, laughed at people living in the dirt, put up signs: No Irish Need Apply.

But by century's turn, the frontier had receded, the Irish rose, built their homes of wood and stone and here you are, a towhead tot, pointing off a porch, Gibson-headed mother Juliana bending near: "Vas is Das?" "Das is Der Moon," her German braiding with the English braiding with the Gaelic of your grandpapa (driven here from famished County Clare). Your mother's family stayed in Germany. Her father was a Prussian officer who laid down his rifle and command. "I can carry it no longer," he declared, left Bismarck to his business, took up farming.

This was the blood that was mixed in you. Your charming Irish father, Dan, amassed a fortune, lost it in The Crash, began again. Sold Morton Salt by the boxcar, elected Town Treasurer over and over, known as a man of integrity. There's that word again, your single most important, what we were to have above all else, integrity.

Juliana, taciturn and not of easy mouth, scrubbed and baked and reared three girls and you. Spoiled you, yes—but she and Dan imparted strict and stern Catholicism (for which a cross was once burned on your lawn).

Still, your spontaneity leaked out: you were a red-caped drummer in the eighth grade when my fourth-grade mother fell in love with you.

Betty kept it to herself, telling not even her best friend, your sister.

•••

By now, an Irish crime lord ran the town with his political machine, and Omaha was full of booze and smoke and dancing girls. And how will a man spare an Irish son from the vices of hooch and tobacco? He made you a promise when you were a lad if you'd keep to yourself and you wouldn't be bad and you'd take not a smoke or a drink and stay clean, you'd get a gold watch when you turned eighteen. And so you did.

(As did we; how many watches now lie broken in our drawers? We all took up the smoke and the drink, living in a house of smoke and ash, smoldering flames, lazy streams of alcohol.)

You were a swimming and a diving champ: your yearbook has you, hands on hips, confident and body proud, though one day at the pool, as you bounced off the board and arrowed your hands, a flash of gold glinted your eye from your wrist: you plummeted down, your gold watch drowned.

•••

Death split your family landscape soon thereafter: pneumonia claimed your favorite sister, you in your twenties and she seventeen. This grief you never spoke to me, though I recall your teared green eye when someone said her name. Alice. I see and hear and smell a fragile dried white rose in a rosewood box.

What are the Irish? What are the movies? You loved Jimmy Cagney, longed to be a G-Man. Clean up Omaha corruption. You took the FBI test and didn't hear for months and then heard no. A crushing blow.

You couldn't fathom why 'til you remembered those two men in that bar, that girlie magazine they offered. You took it, and I see you by dim moonlight, sweat pouring down your Catholic brow from urgent heaving motions: shovel thrusting into earth, burying the magazine to get it out of circulation. Your version of integrity. The FBI thought differently: an easy man to compromise. You studied law instead.

•••

Kinda conceited, Mom said she thought you were. Thought she'd see if she could bring you down a peg or two. She grew in beauty, your kid sister's friend: rich dark hair, dark flashing eyes, when you saw her on group dates, at picnics and the games.

"Sometimes I'd date someone else, just so he wouldn't count on me for dates. But one night, as we said good night, I wore my green coat with the collar—big—I loved that coat—he took me by the collar of that coat and pulled me to him. Never proposed. Told me we were getting married."

No Lent wait for you, but a February wedding on a crystal Midwest day, a wedding breakfast, and a honeymoon in Kansas City on a fifty-cent piece from your coin collection.

You tried to practice law, but your partner was an alcoholic, and in six months you only had two clients, neither of whom paid.

Your voice was good and you loved ballgames so you landed a sportscasting job, broadcast the games with Ronald "Dutch" Reagan.

"Nice guy," you said, tapping your temple, "but not much upstairs."

You and your budding family moved as teams engaged you. Then one day, "He came home, threw his hat on the bed, and said, 'Betty, I've joined the Navy.' Well, yes, it was a shock. But we knew there was going to be trouble. 'Better to enlist,' he said. 'Officers' candidate school. Better salary.'

"Ninety-day wonders, they called them: family men, successful men, they wanted steady men, and in three months he came out second Lieutenant, an Ensign, the gunnery officer."

Not a man behind a little Cagney pistol, now, but a man behind the men behind the big artillery, sailing the Atlantic, the Pacific, four long years of love letters in our attic, and the photographs: you as hero, earnest, crisp in navy whites in the brilliant sunshine of the nineteen forties; you on deck in a bomber jacket, binoculars pressed to your eyes; you and Mom dazzle-eyed in a tropical nightclub when once you got leave; and one of mother, proud and war-bewildered, with the children: Kako five, Pogo three, and baby Tom, fruit of the night at the tropical nightclub.

You told no tales of combat. Your two most vivid stories of the war were born of intuition.

The first happens on a moonless starless night at sea with your radar broken. A craft approaches like a floating German sub; your men want *permission to fire, sir*, but it just doesn't feel like a sub to you, but *better safe than sorry, sir*, if we make a mistake, no one will blame us, *she looks like a sub, sir*, but something tells you not to, so you don't, but all night long you sweat and toss and turn. By dawn's early light you see it is a load of refugees, a boat with some old busted mast that silhouetted like a periscope, and everybody celebrated. It wasn't *Guns of Navarone*, but you saved their lives.

(I think, though, of those huddled on the lifeboat. They knew what they escaped. We took refuge in the Church, refuge in the Army, refuge in career, refuge in solitude, refuge in others, refuge in travel, refuge in alcohol, refuge in food, refuge in art, never knowing what regime we fled.)

Your other story was a dream you had at sea. You dreamt your mother died. When you call, you find out that she had, at just the very time you had the dream. What powers of sight and intuition you could have nurtured.

The souvenirs of war you brought back home belonged to someone else: a German rifle, a Nazi helmet, with Nazi blood on it, and a bullet-riddled flag from your sister ship that looked like the national anthem itself. You named the room in our basement which housed these "Allied Headquarters."

With a black crepe frock from Paris for Mom, back you came, to broadcast games again and a radio show of wisdoms and cheer. My father's voice.

Here's a photo of a you I never knew: with other men standing with a wolf pelt under the wing of a Piper Cub, parka fur flapping, like Gable in a Yukon picture. Dad oh Dad I am desperate to know you.

Back you came, Gibraltar, to rule our grand rambunctious
parliament of dinner, our huge table, edged with eager us, tipping in
the carven chairs, yearning to solve the very sound of the tree falling by
itself in the forest, to come to the Nature of God.

A stone too heavy for us to lift. But we would try.

•••

I see your foot in a green-gold sock rubbing the dog: one of
countless moments of unconscious and anonymous affection. I smell
the evergreen scent of martinis. Great spirit, gentleman, wizard, tree, all
wrapped up in Robert Young, to me. The love, the love, the love, the love
the almost unbearable love.

•••

It seems the feeling was mutual. I found this letter from you among
the family papers:

> May 23, 1959
>
> To my children, all of you—older and younger—
> I felt the urge to tell you I have had a wonderful life. I doubt
> that God has been so good to anyone. He has given to me
> and to you what can be the finest life in this world. Just to be
> Roman Catholic in the United States—the greatest and finest
> country in His world and then to give us as Irene once said.
> Enough, not too rich, not too poor—actually it has been more
> than enough and so has everything else. He has given me so
> always so much more than I could ask—your mother, so much
> more than a wife and mother, so very much more. You—all
> a man could want as a father—I've had more delight and
> satisfaction in these last years than any man deserves. Each
> of you has made such a happy contribution. There is no way
> I can tell you how you have added to my almost total earthly
> happiness—perhaps content is a better word—but you have,

each one of you. Why life has been this way for me and so different for so many millions of others, I don't know. Perhaps because the Lord has made me an instrument by which you can and must contribute yourselves to His world—not all of you in the Religious Life as you have done, Kako, but in distinct and separate ways. Each must find his or her own. But I want each of you to know that you had a happy—and sometimes bewildered Father. It has been a wonderful life thanks to God— your mother and you—Dad.

•••

If only we could stop the story here.

The Old Pew

I did not know we all had different fathers, that I was on
the sunny slope of daughterhood, that my brothers chilled in his
mountainous shadow.

•••

Dad's working seven nights a week. We're alone with Mom. No fun.
Donna Reed shakes no cocktail shaker. Smokes don't screen her from
Mary and Jeff. When Dr. Stone's gone, she doesn't serve bendy fish
sticks and canned peas on worm-green plates in flicker blue light on
black kitchen table.

•••

Mom only tells sad stories like Dad gone in the War or guys way
back in our family connecting the telegraph or her grandpa living in cold
sod house. No games, just boring.

I never want to be a mother. All day stay indoors, do laundry,
sew, with only people who cut their knees, fracture their skulls or be a
horrible mean daughter like me which how could I be so mean to her she
loves me and takes care of me. And all those children of birth defects to
raise money for.

But so boring. I want to be thinking of interesting things, like do
you ever get sick of your body? I do sometimes, dragging it around. It
would be fun to just think all the time.

Feet are good, though, to get around and swim and slide. Also
hands, who let out your mind to write and draw. And eyes to read and
see hands and who are your parents. Also you can cross them, but
careful they might stick.

Mostly I get tired of body not fast like mind. A wish come true if
it ever did because then never wait for a bus. Or think of a drawing,

there it's on paper. But going so fast, you might have to sleep for a month. Boring.

Dying, leave your body. To God if you're good. Hell if you're bad. In Heaven all you do is look at God all day and be happy, but hope there's other stuff to do.

•••

By the following spring, Pogo's left the seminary, transferred to college, and received his gold Omega watch for not smoking or drinking until his eighteenth birthday. As we all will, he makes up for it. After a scrape with a parked car some years hence, he'll stop drinking altogether.

Tom is a high school senior, recovering from a devastating shock. His two closest friends are in a horrible car crash. His best friend dies; his friend Paul is paralyzed. Tom visits him in the hospital and gets to know Paul's kid sister Linda. Tom himself was supposed to be in that car, but changed his plans. The thought haunts us all.

In 1959, Skip turns ten, needs thick glasses, lowering his social status, but upping his grades. He scores in the nighty-eighth percentile in Stanford Achievement Tests. Genius.

Jim, five, is regularly wetting his bed.

Mom's giving and attending more luncheons and coffee parties. "I don't like to go out to lunch on the same day I am having a party," she says in one letter, "...but Anna was here yesterday and the house is all set and I'll skin anyone alive who doesn't keep it that way!"

•••

Don't skin me. I do love to help a party, set olives out, scrub bathroom sink with Comet, put out dinky soaps of fans or shells and velvet towels that don't work but look nice. Polish silver from corner cupboard which feels like weird chalk to my hands. Make baby sandwiches of cucumbers, bread of no crust, paprika for color. Blue Nun Mom pours. A magazine told Mom to spray your phone with perfume so that too. Fill shamrock swan with cigarettes and lickety-split the front door rings. Me and my brothers and sister smile. "Such lovely manners!" people always say. Take their coats on our backs upstairs. Big party, leftover Swedish meatballs. Bridge club, tomorrow eat bridge mix. When I was little I thought they made a bridge of cards and how did they keep it up? Mom says it's just the name. But still I don't know how a real bridge keeps up.

Sometimes me and Mom make bread, white flour hands, sweet-boing-yeast smell, mix dough, knead dough, punch dough down, over and over. Mom says we're part of the long trail of women doing the same thing, centuries, centuries, making bread for centuries. We both feel old, old, old.

Sometimes she cleans out her drawers, gives me apple blossom cologne she doesn't use or old red purse or circle pin she doesn't want.

In my family lots of times it doesn't matter if you are a boy or girl, we are all even. Dad says I can be anything I want when I grow up. But I would like to solve this because I am not perfect to my mother but get mad sometimes.

The chief thing of boys is be brave, but I can too. I cut my finger open to be blood brothers with David I played doctor with, but now he won't be any more, but tells me to get out of here.

It's good to be a girl so you can cry which I don't know what I would do if I couldn't.

•••

Mom's an active member of the hospital auxiliary, Sodality of Mary, the Military Academy Mother's Club, and her alumnae association, and she's on the board of the Variety Club Auxiliary.

She wants less us and more social life.

And yet how I want to stay here in the old pew of the fifties—rigid, dark, uncomfortable, but familiar. Varnished, old incense, something wrong, but so subtle you could forget about it, push it down with Oreos, ignore it walking to school, drink fresh air, distracted by birds.

•••

My way to school is good to me. You go the way of the creek. There's abundance of trees and steep-windingly path, which is best. Or you can take the forty-six gray cement steps right to the green rail foot bridge.

Once Skip raced me down. He took the path and me the steps. I was winning and jumped the last three down but landed on my ankle to sprain it. For the first time I got crutches. Your arms get sore but you feel like a little house walking around. But to beat Skip was worth crutches.

I always anyway like the path better. With dining room table the creek is my best place. A million birds, like mallard ducks and ducklings, or pheasants make sounds like Tin Lizzie. No fox or deer or bear or dinosaur but at our penny-color creek you can pretend.

Step the stones across, but take green rail bridge when you can't, like knobby ice or flood, once up to the sixteenth step. You didn't know where was the bridge. Also once under it Nicky Devin found a lady's dead body murdered there. He said.

I get tardy sometimes because it's so pretty and quiet. Not like family and not like school. Maybe a baby bird fell out of his nest, needs breads and milk.

Cross street, climb The Big Hill. Pull on trees to get up in winter because it's slippery as a frog. In spring, speckle-green. In fall red paint-brush sumac. On top, turn around. Blue trees, blue city way far off.

Trees will not call you names or trip you or make fun, but now get going.

Montana, Day Four: On the Raft

Up early, a bit of yoga on the rocky beach—stretching, thanking the body for that horseback ride.

Mike fries up huckleberry pancakes over the campfire, and after the splatter ware is washed in the river (with my handy camp soap) and rinsed in boiling water, he and Jack show us how to pack the dry bags— tightly rolling things we won't see until the end of the day, things that shouldn't get wet: sleeping bag, air mattress, tent, pajamas. Push, push, push. Cram in as much in as you can, then roll the top over and over and clip the clasp.

Inflating the rafts is an arduous task I leave to prowessy young men.

Holding the manual pump with the handle squarely in his chest, the victim thrusts his upper body up and down, filling the raft with his vigor for an exhausting fifteen minutes, trying to ignore his huckleberry pancakes, until he just has to give the next guy a chance.

They also inflate a one-person pontoon, which will transport more goods and offers personal fun for Jack, who has never tried one before. Lauren eyes it like a Maserati. She wants to get in on the act.

Most of us—though not Jim and his sons (sigh)—pull on life jackets. We clamber into the ungainly fat yellow rafts laden with everything we will use, consume, wear, and recline on in the next five days. Three sprightly fly fishing rods wag merrily. After yesterday's workout, we're definitely ready to float.

Mike captains one raft with Don, Domenic, and Derek. Jack mans the pontoon, and Jim captains our raft, seating Ro on the left, me on the right, and Lauren in the prow.

"The rafts are self-bailing," he says, handing out paddles. "Whatever water gets in will go out through special channels in the floor. River's a little higher than usual this year, but we'll go through some rock gardens."

Good. They sound so lovely. I don't want to miss them.

"Keep one foot in and one foot out of the raft, but pull both feet in when we go over rapids."

This is the sum total of instruction we receive.

Did he say rapids? Ro and I look at each other. They called it a float, right? Neither of us needs or wants the thrill of shooting rapids.

Before we can utter a word, we've suddenly shoved off into the swift river. Almost immediately both rafts are plunging toward a low-hanging, jutting mass of dead pine on the shore.

"Pull, pull!" shouts Jim.

I pull with all my strength, but we zoom straight toward the jabby wood.

"Duck! Duck!"

I cram down low as I can to protect my eyes and win a long bloody scrape down my right arm.

Past the trees, we find two fly rods are decapitated, we're all raked over by sharp branches.

"My god—Lauren's overboard!" She's been cast off and is tumbling swiftly downstream toward the other raft. Mike reaches out.

"Got her!"

He hefts her aboard. This will be Jim's Story Tarp pictograph tonight.

Jim offers us a swig of what the boys call "num-num," named for both senses of the word. This mingling of vodka and fruit punch serves as their navigational fluid. I take some—trying to avoid the thought that not only has this turned into rafting not floating, but that our principal navigators are drinking.

I've hardly swallowed when "Pull!" shouts Jim.

The river is rushing us straight at a rocky outcropping—

Wham!

We bump into it, grab the handles, hang on, swirl a swift 360. No one hurt or dislodged. I'm the kid who got carsick riding reverse in the back of our finny Plymouth Stationwagon. I wept on elevators as a baby.

I screamed a Ferris wheel to a complete stop at age seven because I hated the sensation and had to get off.

I don't like this. At all. But I can't think about this now because we're suddenly bumping in shallows. Thud. Now we're stuck. On slippery rocks.

"Welcome to your first rock garden," says Jim.

This is a *garden*?

"We'll have to portage," he says.

Portaging sounds so simple—lift your boat over areas too shallow to ride, but the raft is as heavy as the finny Plymouth, and the rounded rocks underfoot are designed to flummox your ankles.

Suddenly, Ro slips, falls, her ankle wedged under the raft. Oh God, no. Please, Rocks, let go! Don't snap her ankles! Raft, don't go over her back! Which is just what she fears.

We manage to get her to her feet, her ankle sore, but walkable. She's visibly shaken. I walk even more gingerly than before—sometimes holding the raft, but more often not, since even in the shallows the current pulls the heavy raft faster than I can comfortably walk.

This is so much work.

Ro has a good deal of canoe experience under her webbed belt, but not I.

A few years ago I did take a six-week kayak class, though, and happily (as with my horseback riding class), some of the instruction starts coming back—keeping the window between your arms on the paddle and twisting your torso to go with it. Don reminds me to keep my wrist straight through the stroke. Like the fly fishing, I guess an "unbroken" wrist is par for the wilderness. I just hope it remains unbroken.

•••

We tangle through several more areas on this narrow, swift and twisty river, trying to get to the Big Prairie ranger station, where they promise Tang and cookies. It's amazing what little carrot it takes to inspire work, and how welcome solid ground beneath our feet sounds.

We have several minutes to appreciate the wide mountain-backed prairie and its scolding prairie dogs popping up and down. The long trail to the ranger station gives Ro and me needed sotto voce "Holy Mackerel!" time. Mackerel will be increasingly sanctified as the days unfold.

At last we reach the old wooden ranger station. A tattered picture of Bob Marshall himself is tacked to the wall. Lover of the outdoors and independently wealthy, Bob founded and funded the Wilderness Society, among other accomplishments. Though he died early at age thirty-eight, Bob's efforts and those of the society led to the Wilderness Act, which legally defined wilderness. Congress passed it in 1964, and well over 100 million acres are now protected. We owe this man a lot. He's the father of wilderness preservation. He's why we can be here at all.

The rangers are out of Tang, a funny disappointment. There is lemonade, though, and a package of Chips Ahoy. And the last latrine for the next five days. We postpone going, waiting as long as possible to bid farewell to such luxury.

A strapping young woman hands Mike a paper.

"Here's today's river report."

Mike looks it over. "Okay, good."

I peer over his shoulder.

"The Next Seven Known Hazards."

I try to make sense of this chilling title. *Next* means coming right up. *Seven*. Oh my God. Seven more? *Known*. New ones may have formed since the report was filed. Hazards. The official name for the hellsticks, rockpiles, logjams, and other obstructions we faced. Below this chilling title are suggestions for traversing each one: Keep right. Head down the middle. Bear left, but then sharp right—the fourth hazard comes up quick.

And there's no getting out. There's no leaving. There's no "I'm done." There's no "I didn't sign up for this." There's only "heave ho, back in the boat, you landlubber, you."

How precious a wood-seated, Ur-odored, hand-tended outhouse can feel.

Back down the trail, the ironic Chips Ahoy shift uneasily with the stomach's taking-up of duty. Un-go-back-on-able commitment. Stop thinking about hazards. Anticipating hazards when you don't know navigation sucks the strength out of your muscles like a malted up a straw.

Feet, it will do you no good to shake.

We shove off. Derek is now our prow man. Lauren has joined Mike in the raft ahead and Domenic has switched with Jack. He wants to try the pontoon. I can't even think of safety for these young ones.

Immediately the first hazard springs up like a dragon in a Japanese Noh play. Huge rock to the left, smaller rock to the right. We're supposed to swerve away from them altogether, but there is no controlling the river. Jim's frenzied "Pull! Pull!" is useless. We haven't the strength.

We are suddenly jammed into a cliché, between the Rock and the Hard Place, which cannot be even dwelt upon because there's a sickening POP and the back of the raft is filling with river.

"Get to the front of the boat!" shouts Jim and my body has not yet processed it is in danger or perhaps *it* has but *I* have not and I scramble to the front dimly grasping that if I'd stayed in back, I would have swamped the raft and all our goodies and—don't think about that. The body did respond and got up front.

But we're still stuck between these rocks. How do we get out? We shimmy the raft, we shake, we lunge and lump and at once: release—but we can't relax because we have to think about Mike's raft behind us and waving them away from the rocks and now we're spinning like a Disney teacup. And our raft is leaking.

There are brief intervals where we can catch our breath and have beauty take it away. Rounding a gentle bend in the river, we see ahead of us, perfectly silhouetted against a sandy cut bank, the great mounded back of a shore-exploring black bear. The boys want to go closer.

"Let him have his territory," says Jim.

Ro and I and Don agree, not out of fear, but respect for this stately creature who deserves the run of his world free from the burning eyes of curiosity. But the boys in the other raft paddle close enough to scare him straight up the bank. It is beautiful and sad to watch him clamber up to the bristled treeline edging at the clifftop.

Inky little waterfowl pepper the shallows; killdeer and pipers squeak and seesaw to distract us from their nests.

Ro changes place with Don—she is now in Mike's firmer, non-popped, not leaky raft.

We've surmounted but three of the seven hazards.

•••

The river is higher this year, due to more snowmelt. Lots more. The most snow in fifty years, we learn, therefore the highest, fastest river in fifty years.

The areas Jim calls "rock gardens" sound as lovely and meditative as "float on the river" (which I now know means "Get Buzzed and Shoot Some Rapids.") But I quickly learn that "rock gardens" is Montanan for "Get Out and Walk Your Boat." Or "Bid Farewell to a Working Ankle." Or perhaps "You Don't Need Two Functioning Knees, Do You?"

The accurate translation is: grab a little handle on the side, lug a mountain of equipment-laden raft over the few tablespoons of water coating the rocks just enough to make them treacherously slippery, and time it so that you proceed neither faster nor slower than your team, because the raft will pull you cracking to your knees if you're not fast enough; and if you're too fast, you'll pull the others down and all the while the rocks ogle your knees and ankles like hyenas eye a limping zebra.

In truth, it is a meditation, because your mind cannot swerve from the task at hand, or you might make a deadly mistake.

That's what I don't like. Seems the trip is all about avoiding damage—to your team, yourself, your raft. Never liked the verb "avoid."

•••

What I appreciate about Jim as captain is his enthusiasm and his praise when we have coasted right down the middle of the silver V.

"Woo-woo!" we wave our paddles overhead. It's a thrill when you get it right.

And we're here, surviving, spending time with family. I have a shimmer memory of our departed brother. It all goes by so fast.

"I can't believe I have waited so many years to do this," Ro says. "Should have started in my thirties."

Then the other raft rams us, tossing me backwards into the water.

When I get my breath back, I find it's fairly shallow, so I get my bearings and rise carefully on the slippery rocks. Don pulls me back in, reminding me of the stability of fireman's grip, grabbing forearms, not hands.

Twelve miles of paddling on our first day. Soaked and shivering, we pull the rafts ashore at our second campsite and run to pee. In my chosen spot I spy a long elk femur. Elegant, yet disturbing. Can't say why.

Let's get into dry clothes. Unroll the dry bags. Oh no—water has gotten into some of them, soaked some clothes, and the repeated impacts smashed open the canister of Slap Ya Mama spice powder, which has pasted itself all over my new jacket. Oh well. At least we're on dry land, and here's a bag that didn't get wet.

Climb into warm dry clothes and set up camp. Out comes the single malt.

"Something hurts," says Jim, tapping his back. I take a look—he's bleeding from a branch stab unfelt in the moment. I clean it up and dab on ointment.

Beauty, camaraderie, cooperation. But also Wilderness.

I am a soul who relishes choices, who tries 'em on like shoes and collects 'em like handbags. One reason I didn't have children is they profoundly curtail decades of choices.

But here there is no choice. You don't want to get back in the leaky raft. You want out. The only choice you have is the one you already made: to join these people on this journey. Even if it's stressing and distressing and painful and frightening. Even if it should never have been asked of you. Even if you and Montana speak two different languages. Risk is oxygen to Montanans.

No matter what you think, no matter how you feel, short of an airlift, there's no way to get where we're going except to propel ourselves through the river, whatever it brings.

Let go, here at the fragrant warm campfire. I'm grateful to see these glowing family faces, but look at that gouge in Don's leg. Ro's ankle is blue and swollen. That has to hurt. Such wicked scratches down Jim's arm. How did Mike and Jack get so cut up? Though I'm sore and fatigued, seeing my relatives bloody and battered weakens my knees.

But we made it. Enjoy the comforting stew and hot biscuits Mike whipped up in a flash. Join this lively conversation, watch event and shock and effort congealing into stories larded with good-natured ribbing.

And this unfamiliar brilliance in your body? The tingle of survival. She admits this more easily than the rest of you. You whisper "stop mewling" to yourself.

Besides, we're two days at this campsite. Tomorrow's a full day of rest.

After dinner, Jim hands Domenic a book.

"Read us a story."

"Naw, Jim." Reading aloud, so easy for us, is to him a scary set of rapids.

"Ah, come on, Dom. This guy's a funny writer."

Domenic looks at the book. "They Shoot Canoes, Don't They?" Patrick McManus.

"Read us 'History of the Tuttle Lake Expedition.' You'll like it."

"Oh, that's a good one," says Mike.

"Yeah, read it!" calls Jack.

Domenic haltingly begins, and then relaxes with every laugh he gets. By the time he finishes, he can ham it up with the best of us and we are all aching with laughter.

•••

The evening winds down. There still some good stars shooting.

Don and the kids decide to sleep out under the stars. I want to see them unmeshed myself. Ro wants me to stay with her in the tent. It's still unclear to me why.

"I've come so many miles to see real stars, Ro. I want to. You camp all the time."

Ro has a knack for viewing superb celestial events. She's always describing a sky fluttering with showering meteors or double rainbows or extraordinary planetary convergences, eclipses, balls of green lightning. I just want a good look at the night sky.

"Sorry." I pull my sleeping bag out of the tent.

"You will be if you get wet," she grumbles. She's miffed, but it's our only spat on the trip—the rest of the time, when I was uncomfortable or panicky, she was in a good way, and vice versa.

In rare moments of resting heart rate, it's clear the splendor of the terror and the trauma is the teamwork—well-experienced and strong family members all doing their best to assist and protect each other. Utterly depending and dependent on each other.

Burglar

By 1960, my protectors are gone. (Not Dad, but he's working a lot.) Every life holds such changes, but in a large family they come earlier. "People come and go so quickly here."

I write to Kako, my maternal surrogate. I could always make Pogo laugh—our senses of humor were similar: quirky, verbal, but he wasn't writing letters. Mom once described me as a feminine version of him, but I know she likes him better. Tender Tom of baby rabbit fame is at St John's University now. Though an hour's drive, it feels thousands of miles away. As does my self-esteem.

I chalk notes to Dad, in Burma Shave ways reminding him to take his vitamins. In his square letters he chalks a rhyme back; all of our worded affection erased with a pass of a wet paper towel in my mother's red hand.

Skip gets my jokes, he's smart, but he doesn't like me. He always tries to prove how smart he is, so I have to prove how smart I am, so he can prove I'm not. I can't just relax. We take turns watching the Littles or setting the table, but at night when we are screaming at each other over who will wash and who will wipe the red, red counters and the gray linoleum surrounding all around us, I see ourselves in the black night windows like the sun will never shine again and I hate it. I hate to be a prisoner of the dishes on a never-ending night.

I have to toughen up, find some extra love. Where?

One whole week when I am eight and Ro is two, each night in the streetlit dark of our shared room, I pull on cap and bandit-kerchief and roar into her little slatted crib, "I'm a burglar! I'm going to get you!" Then I step back, whip off my disguise, step forward as myself, her champion.

"I'll save you!" I bend back, make the sounds of struggle, toss the cap, swoop her up and tell her she is safe because of me.

This is not a game. I do it to scare her and to save her, so she'll look up to me.

I still feel the rawness of my burglar throat.

•••

"I'll protect you from any bad thing," I said, so she'd love me. But *I* was the bad thing. What makes me be so mean? Worse than Skip. Why even feel bad feelings?

Like I love animals so much so why sometimes when I pick a kitten up do I want to squeeze and squeeze it is so cute which would hurt it which I would never do so why want to? This feeling comes, but lucky not my hands but makes me scared to pick up kittens.

Then there are bad feelings people make you feel on purpose, which why? To look at me you maybe see a reason to call me names but why? I never hurt them. I say, "Sticks and stones may break my bones but names will never hurt me," but go to Confession. You lied.

I get scared to be so mean to my little sister or mad at Mom who loves me because what if Russia got mad at us who hates us?

This scary feeling is like hearing "Tornado coming." Go down the basement. Take candles, radio, deck of cards.

The tornado blows up houses stores schools churches. Many die.

So with Russia I think how I get tornado mad. What if they blew us up? Worse than the worst Twilight Zone. Worse than my nightmare parade.

At school we have drills to our gym with gray rooms of food and water. But what if we're home? In our basement we have only three tomato jars and one peaches that were there fifty years.

If they blew us up everything would be gray and gone and terrible.

It's hard work not to think of this. If it did I would try to be brave and help the way of a good Girl Scout. The only person to get me through this would be God. My giant wish is He would not let this happen. But He let me be mean to my sister and mad at my mother so maybe not. It's hard to know what's in His will. But I would keep trying because who else?

They might not kill us, though, but take over. Skip says no matter what I say, they'd say, "You lie!"

"Then I'd say I hate Brussels Sprouts and they wouldn't give me any."

But they despise priests and nuns, which spells trouble for Kako. Me, too if I become one.

•••

So it's a joyful night when the Catholic takes the White House. Now we're talking. How great, living in a country that never lost a war, in Minnesota, which was North in the Civil War so it never lost, and now a Catholic president. Winners all the way.

No doubt I bake a celebratory batch of cookies. I learned to bake around this time, with help from Mom, Betty Crocker, Girl Scouts, my E-Z Bake oven, and a child's cookbook from the Bookmobile—oh those carnival cookies, loaded with coconut, butter, and powdered sugar.

I want to bake so urgently that I beg Mom to ask neighbors for cups of sugar when we run out. She won't, though. I've written elsewhere of the rewards of baking: not just fingerfuls of dough, and the pick of the just-baked cookie litter, but the love and attention of the family. It surpassed even poetry for garnering praise—feeding my need into their need, which fed back into mine.

For Mom is making the world a better place: raising money for children with defective hearts, flying them in from India and Africa and South America.

•••

You scoured the globe, Mom, for children with punctured valves and malformed chambers, who engaged you in a way our bickering, our jockeying, our accidents, our falling grades, our pain, our health did not. The irony was lost on you: healing the hurt hearts of strangers' children by hurting the hearts of your own.

All along, you said you were an awful mother, and, "This house is a mess, I never get caught up." We learned your heaving purple sighs were cues for us to say, "No, no you are a wonder mother! The messy house is all our fault, hot dog hash, canned spinach are delicious. You look pretty smell the Chanel where you going?"

When you are gone, looking for your soft cheeks, deep brown eyes, high hair in your vanity mirror, drawing my finger through the fine snow left by your powderpuff, whispering into your lipstick, hugging your puffy chiffons. You *are* Donna Reed. Come back, I'll be good.

Holding postcards to a landscape blocks the view, yet we do it all the time.

Who are you and who am I? What is America, what is TV?

Family Portrait

Any child knows the features of her family like Braille, but describing them is challenging and slippery. At what age? Hair changes, teeth get knocked out, bodies swell and shrink. Also, what if I'm wrong? Being right was imperative in my family, especially with lynx-eyed brother Skip eager to pounce on my slightest mistake. Better look at a photograph just to be sure. Given the twenty-year span from oldest to youngest, it was so rare for the whole family to be together that there are only two or three of all of us.

This snapshot was taken in 1961. Before Kako took her final vows, they let her come up to the lake with us one last time.

Why are we standing outside the cabin not in Keds and fishing pants, but all dressed up? Mom wears a white pleated skirt and heels; both Dad and Skip wear suits and ties. Ro and I are in dresses, straw hats, and patent leather T-strap party shoes. Kako (Sister Eileen, by then) is in full Benedictine habit, Jim's in a decorative sweater. The older boys sport short-sleeved white shirts like Mormons. Of course. We're off to Mass. It's why there wasn't time to take a better shot.

We're not a bad-looking bunch—heart-shaped faces, regular features. Dad supplied our broad foreheads, Mom our softly pointed chins, and to most of us, her flashing dark McCreary eyes. Dad's eyes were mutable—hazel-gray-green; Skip and Tom got those.

Our soft Irish complexions tend to pink and rosacea, though come summer, some of us are champion tanners like Dad. Only Skip suffered from acne.

Most of us, as the old song goes, were built for comfort, not for speed—short-waisted, short-necked, from the German side, none too tall, squarish, with flat butts (a word we were not allowed to use).

Ro and Jim got a bit more of Mom's dainty joinery. She had fine cheekbones and was delicate in wrist, hand, and ankle.

Mom was always proud of her hands. She loved to glove them in kid, which she bought for a song since she had to buy sample-size.

These little hands were dexterous at typewriter, sewing machine, and cigarette-lighter.

In this picture, though, they are crossed over her womb as if to say, "No more." She's gotten her figure back after delivering Ro four years earlier, but looks as she often does: a saint at the stake, exhausted, resigned. "Lord, deliver me."

Dad's Gable looks have softened into a paunchier, more avuncular look. His hands are square and capable but are not builder's hands. He's not interested in tools, except as they help catch fish.

Kako is smiling. With a more confident personality, she would have been pretty. But except around us, she's somewhat withdrawn, which makes her face look plain. She and Skip and I share doughiness. At nine and eleven, he and I are clearly overweight. But brains were always more important than bodies in this family.

Pogo and Tom are both good-looking—Tom light and Pogo dark. Military training at their high school keeps them in good shape, but their looks also grow from personality—the eldest boy's birthright pottage of confidence, his younger brother's earned by focused concentration.

Shy-smiling Jim is the most straightforward, yet vulnerable little presence—by this time he has already been hospitalized twice—for a hernia, and for biting his nails into near gangrenous infection.

Cute as she is, you can't see Ro's face—she's turned to me. Whatever the question, she's not looking to Mom for the answer.

We didn't need the corrections other children did—nobody needed braces, and only Skip needed heavy black-rimmed glasses for his flicky gray-green eyes. Our corrections came in other forms.

But though it is not evident here, the feature you'd notice most about us at any age is that intensity I mentioned—that warmth of gaze, that curiosity, that listening interest. One of the family jewels.

And here at the lake there is so much to hear.

Up to the Lake

"Can we go to New York or Grand Canyon or Yellowstone with bears like Walt Disney or someplace kids talk about?"

"I think we'll go up to the lake this year," every year Dad says, like he just thought of it. But always we're glad we came.

Green duffel bag, footlocker of Dad in the War. Stuff everything in. Fishing rods and life jackets pile in the hall.

Next day "All hands on deck! Up 'n' at 'em!" Pack car. Make baloney sandwiches. Mom can't wait to get to Heaven to see how many sandwiches in her whole life she made. Oreos or maybe I made chocolate chip. Fill thermoses, one Kool-Aid, one coffee. Count noses, drive around the block to see what we forgot. Yes, my fishing hat, run back, get it, drive away.

In the Car

Say the Rosary for safety. Then Hangman, Ghost or Alphabet—get all the alphabet in a row from signs. Or read Burma Shave.

Or play Horse. Five points for every horse, twenty for a white horse and cemetery wipes you out. I don't mind losing. I just like seeing horses.

Get hungry, eat baloney sandwich. Go to the bathroom in gas station.

Back in the car, sing *Tom Dooley, Jimmy Crack Corn and I Don't Care, Michael Row the Boat Ashore, Ants Go Marching* or Christmas Carols, just for pretty harmony.

How many more miles. A lot. Skip punches you for no reason, pulls your hair. "Ow!"

Dad says, "Settle Down." Mom pours him coffee.

Some can read in a car but I get sick. But maybe Skip once is nice to let me sit by the window. I like it to take every strength to open your eyes in the wind, flapping cheeks and elbow triangle.

Dixie cup of Kool-Aid. Ro crawls back, curls next to you asleep. Farmers, kneeling cows, rows and rows of corn fan open and shut. Soon, dark. Drive more. Million dead bugs on the windshield.

But then a turn and another. Stop. We're there.

•••

Everything quiet from no sound of windows. Dad keeps on headlights and someone runs and gets the cabin key from Mr. Walters. Air is piney and chirpy of crickets.

Get in pajamas and bed. Like Christmas, but you'll be opening days not presents. So dark you can't tell if your eyes are open or closed. Sleep.

At the Lake

Next morning your nose wakes you up. Pancakes! Brothers stuff them in whole. Eat a stack, then outdoors to see how everything still is.

Check thermometer. Seventy-two? Not yet. Catch frogs. Nickel for each for bait for bass.

Look again. Sixty-eight. Boo.

Play horseshoes with round iron sound.

Look again. Yay! Seventy-two degrees! Quick get in your bathing suit! (Jim calls it his swimming panties!)

Pull out purple towels. Blow up beach ball. Mom, please, it's seventy-two? She smiles, ties on her big straw hat and down the steps to the lake we go. Coppertone. At the end we will have a tan contest of arms.

Cold. Inch in. Skip splashes you. Splash back. He tries to push you down but you get him first. Down he goes! Yay! He sputters he will get you. Underwater he swims. Where is he? Suddenly your leg's grabbed down you go.

Water Tag, King of the Raft, donk the beachball on everyone's head. I can stand on my hands under water and do Deadman's Float.

Jim can't come out too far so piggyback him. Everything is easy in the water.

Sometimes hold breath, go way down on muddy bottom, then float up. Maybe how it feels to die, soul rising up to God. But who to ask? Everyone who knows is dead.

Come out. Ro's building toad castle.

Freezing. Run up wood stairs to little house of two showers connected to tiny store where you hear Dad talk over the wall about minnows. Later go back to buy Salted Nut Roll, but now shower. Back to cabin for Braunschweiger sandwich.

After lunch, fishing with Dad. Just me and Dad this time. Nobody else.

The Hook in the Heart

Easy it enters. Steady now, rocking from the dock to the ribby, chipped, unbailed bottom of the don't forget the tacklebox, the Coppertone, the pipe tobacco. Two pairs of shoes full of feet: a steady canvas gummy-bottom pair, two twirling bump-toed Keds.

Bronze-red upturned outboard, sleek as a Zippo, as his Remington shaver, paddle dip paddle dip, tipping the propeller in. Gasoline rainbow spreading on the surface and the pull and the pull like a lawnmower cord and the mixmaster buzz and the gurglechurned duckweed, shoreline, treeline, timeline shrinking in the sightline.

Shadowbottom clouds, the tremendous clouds in the breezeblue sky and the snap of the sun on the wake on the waves we make as we fly through the watery way to a shadowy bay: "Looks promising today."

Holler over the outboard motor, noisy as another set of siblings: persistent permanent, clamoring, yammery. Finally stops and the anchor drops.

Ploosh. Easy it enters. Lapping water. Softly tapping reeds. Tackle's metal melody. Plunge in the bucket. Slithery wriggly minnows as lively as fingers.

"Hook him under the dorsal fin, so he can swim."

The Keds curl. The pierce of the hook in the heart.

Clickety whizz of the casting reel, ploop of the bobber. Red and white and red and white reflected. Great wide glassy lake of nothing to be done.

•••

Circling. Settling silt. Haloes round our shadows on the water.

Skeetling. Skeetling. Redyellow flash. Blackwing.

Scratch of a match. Crackle of tobacco. Draw through the stem the flute blue sigh. Wind through pines. Dragonfly.

Easy it enters. Shadow twist light. Love twist loss. Twist.

Lake Ways

FISH HOUSE

Go to gray shack fish house. Dad knocks them out so they don't feel a thing. Scale them with crispy ringy sound, which they fly in hair eyes mouth like Ro's little fingernails.

Cut off head and tail and slit them open. I always have scaled but never yet slit.

Inside all different shiny lumps of yellow blue white red gray.

Sometimes he opens his stomach to see what he ate. Or a million of eggs.

Put good in foil and bad in newspaper and throw out.

One time Skip put fishhead in this iron squeezy and turned and turned 'til bones cracked and eyes popped out which he threw them at me. But I threw them back.

Back to cabin. Mom fries the good new fish in cornmeal. Eat them up.

AFTER DINNER

After dinner Mom and Dad always go fishing alone. They never catch anything so why go but they do. Sit around, play Monopoly, Kool-Aid, Oreos.

Or squirt gun fight or draw Band-Aids and scars on all the ladies in the magazines. Or try to read in your room or draw, but cabin has no ceilings, only roof and rafters so Skip throws sopping wet Kleenex over the wall. Throw it back, but once it hit Dad coming in the door.

Get in bed. Giggle and whisper and Skip's tennis shoe comes flying over.

"Settle down, that's enough."

Look out at moths wanting in or pine knots above and see things there, horsehead or hamburger, like looking at clouds till you fall asleep. Worst is if a mosquito hums right in your ear all night who won't stop till you smash him in your own face. Which hurts but then you can sleep.

GOING INTO TOWN

Go in little town for laundry and souvenir store of Indians or dime store with beautiful horse statues. Here are other souvenirs, but don't buy. Jim's tomahawk said Made in Japan.

Then pile in grocery sacks, duffle of laundry, stop at Dairy Queen and drive back to cabin except this one time.

THIS ONE TIME

This one time we got our laundry and Dad said, "We have our clothes. Let's drive to Canada." Yay!

First stop, Paul Bunyan and Babe Blue Ox statues. So high his foot was taller than my whole self.

Then Great North Woods to stop at the start of the Mighty Mississippi which you can step on stepping stones across.

Here are real Indians in teepees who I love. They make canoes and clothes I wish I had of feathers and leathers and have pretty skin like Spanish peanuts.

North and north drive into my first foreign land. Get all new money but most foreign is Juicy Fruit Gum in French.

Go to forts of French Davy Crocketts, but best is mighty beauty of Northern Lights like big gasoline across the sky.

SECOND WEEK

Soon you go home, so slow up.

Set alarm clock of my head to wake early and earlier for more time. Sneak out at blue dawn for sunrise. In rain, watch rings and wrinkles of gray water sitting on the old gray dock in your Girl Scout poncho.

All of the sudden, last day. Arms together in a row. Jim wins for brown sugar tan. Last pancakes. Last boiling water to wash dark blue glasses and flower plates I miss when we go.

Feel sorry for clothes who had vacation of no closets and drawers, just shelves and poles. Stuff green duffle bag.

Tell goodbye to Finnegan the black dog and the swallows in the cliff. Thank your lake for making twice the sky and trees and sparkles of sun like thoughts.

Then Skip squirts you grab your red squirt gun pull out stopper dump your ammo down his back. Good revenge. All his clothes are packed and has to ride in hot car with wet back. Do not sit next to him.

The way home, the same games. See your city with different eyes like you never lived there. The house after vacation is one of my favorites. Quiet, dark, drapes all shut, big mail heap under the slot in the dining room, newspapers. The house rested while we were gone and had no sound but neighbor key and watering plants. It's glad to have us back.

Montana, Day Five: In Camp

The next day we're blessedly staying put. We can actually relax. Don and Jack play chess, Lauren washes laundry, Ro, Jim, and others play cards. Mike is deservedly slung up in his hammock, snoring. Too wired to take out my watercolors, I sit under a tree, reading John Muir and looking up from time to time.

I'm glad I get to the health club regularly and lift weights. In spite of the hours of paddling yesterday and on horseback the day before, I'm not sore.

After a few handfuls of lunch—on the trail it's always snacks: nuts, chocolate, fruit—I do a stupid thing.

Appreciate where you are, I tell myself, and pick up the skinny wire-bound guidebook Jim has at last laid down. The river is sectioned on these pages. These dog-eared pages are the sequence of the maps for our trip.

Big mistake.

The mapmaker has highlighted in pink the locations of multiple upcoming rapids. Oh my God it looks like chicken pox. Okay, okay, calm down. But so many. Look, it's just a few days. You can do this.

Okay, really, how long *is* this trip? I flip to the last dog-ear. The take-out point is here by this big red mark. What's this say? Scout these rapids! Very dangerous. The worst rapids are at the end? Beware. I'd Turn Back If I Were You. My Cowardly Lion tail twitches in my hand.

I try to forget the warning, but it remains a big red throb for the rest of the journey. You're not going to get the hard stuff over and then relax, Irene. The Worst Is Yet To Come.

I won't tell Ro.

Ro worries. I do my best not to worry her. I do my best to remind her how good she is, how smart, how sensitive.

She's dearer and closer than anyone but my husband, and there's no one I'd rather share this trip with. She's the river running through our family landscape, like the Mississippi, starting stepping-stone small, then broadening, uniquely nourishing each of us.

She totally gets girl-fun—loves the occasional trashy movie or a side-by-side dip into Vogue, chatting fashions: the fabulous and ridiculous ones we wore, the ridiculous and fabulous ones now. Laughter with her attains pants-wetting intensity.

You want her with you when you shop. "Check the seams! How often will you really wear that?" She spots the genuine bargain—not something cheap, but quality at a low price.

You want her at your side cooking, too—her palate is like the sensitive perfumer's nose—a specificity nearly acrobatic to behold. Will she make it to the end of the dish with accurate stepping? Of course. She always does.

"Cinnamon, nutmeg, allspice—a bit of coriander. I would have toasted the walnuts, brought up the flavor a bit. Almost anything front to back of the meal can be improved with lemon." She lends her chopping hand and culinary smarts with no ego whatsoever.

She can talk books, theater, art, and human motivation, because she is a deep listener. She knows the little hollow places hurt collects, offers wise advice.

And you surely want her in the wild, for Ro is exquisitely tuned to nature and celestial events: it is she who spots the halo around the moon, the phosphorescent sea creatures, multicolored wings of Aurora Borealis. Hummingbird babies play at her sprinkler; over her shoulder the owl reveals himself. Her cosmic sensitivity yields also a fierce sense of justice that led her to marry a brilliant compassionate criminal defense lawyer who shares the same. This woman asks the deep questions, loves to study wisdom.

But she also carries within her a black leather moto-jacketed maverick. She wanted a tattoo back when no one but sailors got them.

Oh sure, she can drive me crazy with a fear that seems unfounded, or an occasional lack of belief in herself, or the need for some configuration of objects, temperatures, and sensations that must be met or her discomfort will be tooth-clenching.

But I drive her crazy, too, with my own fussy requirements, my name-dropping, my own misgivings about myself.

And Jim and Skip and I are somewhat to blame. She was a trusting and gullible child and we mercilessly hoodwinked her.

"Watch out! It might explode. That's not a horse chestnut. See these spikes? It came from outer space. Aliens sent it to Earth. "

"Don't sing 'Pick a Bale of Cotton!' You don't know what it means? It's offensive and insulting."

Once we'd hooked her, we'd laugh and laugh. "You believed that? We were just kidding!"

We were just terrible.

And of course we were hogging all the dinner table attention (to say nothing of the food), making it nearly impossible for her to get a word in edgewise.

How did Ro turn out so well?

For one thing, she learned to watch. The whack-a-mole shift of demands in a household as large as ours called for quick adjustments. She is a natural artist and her eye has always been sharp.

But on one occasion her combination of innocence and artistry led to a damaging incident.

•••

In a quiet classroom moment, Ro decides to draw her finger. No other paper nearby, she begins the careful pencil sketch on the grocery-bag cover she made to protect her speller. Funny baggy knuckle, curved fingertip, hint of fingernail.

Not every finger, just the one. One, like her, in a twitching hand of siblings.

She shades the sides. She's good at this.

"What does this mean?!" her teacher roars and yanks the book away.

Ro is utterly bewildered. "What?"

"*You* know! Obscenity! Obscenity!"

Ro is marched over the unyielding terrazzo, through the wood and starry glass door into the principal's office.

"Call her parents immediately. I won't have her in my class!"

The call is made; Ro is sent home.

The artist does not understand her crime. Nor does Dad that night. He inspects the evidence.

"What were you drawing, honey?"

She holds up her left index finger.

"What did I do wrong, Dad?"

"Your teacher has a sick mind. She thinks it's a vulgar gesture."

He calls Monsignor Colbert, at *this* time of night. I hear the buzz and murmur of his conversation accelerating into his professional broadcaster thunder.

"That drawing is perfectly innocent. This warped woman is libeling my daughter. If there's one black mark on her record I will sue the teacher, I will sue the school and I will sue the Catholic Church if need be."

Mom pales with embarrassment, yet she too knows her Ro is innocent. The school capitulates.

As for Ro? The teacher's shriek, the public humiliation, the chill of the principal's office, her mother's gasp, her father's fury, and her own molten confusion flow into the muscles of her arm and harden into doubt. Her drawings become tinier and tinier. Unquestionably non-controversial. Unicorns. Daisies. Valentines. An artist exiled from anatomy.

•••

While Ro and her powerful creativity eventually surmounted this, to a large extent we were all brought up exiled from anatomy (particularly our own). And we were brought up to doubt. To doubt ourselves, our impulses.

A Blur of Sins

ONE.

The soul is odd because it has no forward like body or back like mind, just always in the middle of right now.

It gets you to breathe because if it leaves you die. The shape of it is a milk bottle which gets spots from sins. Lucky Confession gets them off but still I wish I would never get any on.

Numbers made me sin.

I like learning most things, which is like making things but you can't touch them but can use them. Sometimes they are fun at the dining room table to say. Like there's a juice in your hands for your fingers to move and not hurt. Or Obet and Kara eat in Hawaii breadfruit. And learn all other people of foreign lands.

Especially I like English. Except not spelling with no sense. All the time I get words wrong on my test that should be right. Like people. Every time I spell the way it sounds she marks me wrong: *pepole*. Always I have to say pe-OP-le when I write it. Also answer. What's that W doing there? I might when I grow up invent an easier spelling way. But I love The Alphabet. Like another parent who always helps me.

But I surely hate numbers. I'm sorry The Alphabet even makes the word. What good are they?

Letters and words are good as the sandbox. You can make anything—prayers, stories, shows, planets. And say what's important, what you feel, like sorry or something.

But no matter how you put numbers together you only get numbers. No number's better than another and you can never make a new one up because somebody already thought up every one up to infinity.

Numbers don't care what you feel, only if you're right. Like Skip. Worst, there's only ever one right answer. Multiply or subtract or anything. They never care how hard you try. It never shows with numbers. Only are you right or wrong. If you're wrong it's horrible. If you're right you're just like everybody else.

And I never can get it right. I have to go to the blackboard and be stupid in front of everyone and the teacher gets mad. I hate arithmetic!

It made me sin. I get sick to think of it.

I had flu and missed a quiz of fractions which I hate so much because they are even littler than numbers. On Friday I came back. Sister was reading the answers out. I knew she'd make me take the test and I would never pass so I started to write the answers down on my desk by the ink hole.

She saw me and got so mad she threw a blackboard eraser at me. The class all opened their mouth. She said she was ashamed at me and made me go to the principal's office.

My principal was ashamed at me too. She called my mom to say she was sending me home early but would not say why but that I would tell when I got there.

Then I had to go home and tell my mom and then my dad. This was the hardest thing to do I ever had in my life, because they were the most ashamed.

"When you cheat you only cheat yourself," said Dad, but it was my sickest feeling ever.

TWO.

Sometimes on my way home from school, after a difficult day, I take the long way home. Woods had their comforts, but I have to envision adulthood, my power. Where?

The Red Owl Grocery Store.

A vast, spacious, orderly, cool kingdom, lined with appealing, colorful packages. Soft music. No cart—I'm shopping for my future. I stroll the aisles like a bride in a lingerie shop, examining the comestibles, assessing their potential to give pleasure, delaying gratification until I allow myself the pinnacle of imaginary transport: the cookie aisle. There I stand in mouthwatering trance, fantasizing growing up and filling my cart with them—even the expensive ones: Mallowmars and Pinwheels—taking them home and devouring whole boxes and bags by myself. (An ambition I later repeatedly fulfill.)

One day, mid-reverie, I have to use a bathroom. Few stores had public restrooms in those days, because people didn't spend hours shopping. When I asked the balding, pencil-behind-the-ear manager, he kindly sent me downstairs to the employee breakroom.

No one is there. Waiting on the lunch table, as if in spotlight: a glistening platter of Danish and a basket for honor contributions. I had no money, but filched a pastry anyway, stuffed it down, peed, scooted back upstairs, spinning with guilt and satiety.

I did this for a week. Then one afternoon in the cookie aisle as I behold my lovelies, I'm startled by a bark at my elbow.

"Did your parents send you to buy something?" The manager's kindly face has twisted to a scowl.

I'm utterly flustered. I never buy anything. It isn't even Mom's regular store—she goes to Super Valu.

"No sir. I thought a store was like church—welcome anytime."

He shakes his pencil at me.

"You're no longer welcome here. What's your parents' phone number?"

I stand thoroughly humiliated as he calls my mother. Lying. Stealing. Real sins. And now denied my solace: fantasy and sweet rolls.

•••

Facing Mom and Dad again. *Aw, honey,* the worst inflection in their repertoire. More excruciate than brimstone.

Not that much love to go around, you know. If you don't toe the line, love, like Oreos, might be snatched by someone smarter, more thoughtful, quicker to please, or downright holier than thou. Someone better at fulfilling Catholic expectations:

Make us proud (but don't be proud, it's a sin). Be good (something you must try to be, not something that you are). Ignore your body (it pulls you into sin and keeps you from sainthood). If you can't feel good, feel guilty.

So voiced and unvoiced guilt juts throughout our landscape: Tom turns his back on baby Jim who then rolls off the bed. Though Jim is uninjured, Tom tortures himself with the thought that because of his carelessness, Jim may yet get ill, go blind, or become mentally retarded. I'm guilty because, according to Skip, my birth caused Dad's heart attack. Bandage-handed Jim feels it's all his fault: "If I'm really good they'll let me keep my fingers." Bedwetting cracked skull skin disease hernia ruptured spleen head cut open eating disorders drinking disease. Spikes and thorns and holy hell of guilt. Feeling bad as a way to feel good. Because then you might be forgiven.

"Pay them back for the sweet rolls from your allowance," Dad concluded. "And don't go back again."

THREE.

But sin is so confusing. One time there was a raffle at my school for pagan babies. You had to bring in books of green stamps to enter and Mom would only give me one, but I stole another. Then I won the prize. A rosary.

To pray for my horrible soul.

FOUR.

Later, I commit sins right in the middle of my confirmation, the sacrament of maturity in seventh grade.

When you are confirmed, you choose a saint's name to add to yours. I select Teresa of the Little Flower, whom I most wish to imitate, and immediately do something she would never do. When the bishop anoints me, I sneak my hand up to the holy oil on my forehead and touch it. The very same Holy Chrism only consecrated, priestly, male fingers are sanctioned to touch. But if The Chrism touched my forehead, why not my fingers?

Then the bishop asks questions of each candidate. After answering, I asked one of my own. (Highly contrary to protocol, this infuriated Skip.)

"If God knows what we are going to do before we do it, why did He make us? Aren't we all just puppets, then?"

Whatever Dad had said did not convince me. I'd asked every teacher, our principal, Father Dudley, and even Monsignor Colburn. Everyone always mumbled something fuzzy about Free Will, which made no sense. We didn't seem free if He knew our future. The bishop had to have an answer.

He murmured the same vague generalities I'd already dismissed.

Wow. Even the most powerful, most religious people didn't know. There was room to look for and find answers of my own.

The following Saturday, standing in line at the confessional, preparing my list of sins (touching Holy Chrism, greed, not honoring my mother and father, anger at my brother, and a host of others) I happened to look up at the line. There stood Mom, Dad, my brothers and sister, and neighbors and strangers. It struck me: Everybody sins. Even Mom and Dad. A comfort almost surpassing forgiveness itself.

Good Grooming

Some mothers spend time with their daughters, teaching them how to care for said precious body. Grooming is passed along as a fun thing, a nourishing thing. Other mothers don't care for themselves or their daughters at all. But a mother who cares for her own grooming and not her daughter's makes a statement.

NAILS

Nail-biting plagued us, from *The Family Journal* competitions to Jim's grievously infected nails.

Mine were no exception. I was a thumb-sucker—gateway drug. John showed me how to bite nails, including toenails. "Like shrimp tails," he said. I went one better by picking, stripping, and nibbling my cuticles as well.

What on earth prompts this painful, unattractive behavior? It is the sensation that your nails and cuticles are not smooth and should be. Like you.

You don't go at it like a cutter, thinking, "Gosh, I'd like to make myself bleed," though that frequently ensues.

No, the thinking runs: "If only I pull off this little protrusion, my fingers will be smooth." Makes perfect sense, except that it always takes your fingers into rougher territory, which calls for more rigorous action, and more, and more, resulting in the shock of blood, which brushes your dingy school blouse, making everything worse. All the while the twist in your subconscious whispers: if I hurt myself enough, I'll stop hurting.

HAIR

When I was small, Mom enjoyed spending time on my hair. For special occasions she'd tear small strips from used-up sheets, wind locks of my fine damp blonde hair around them, and tightly knot them to hold the curl as it dried. I would knobbily sleep on them and wake in the morning with golden ringlets.

At that stage they meant more to her than to me—evidenced by the day I smuggled scissors into nap time, and having tired of sleeping on bumps, cut whacking great hanks off my head. And while I had no idea how radical my action was or how long it would take to rectify, I instantly had a sense of wrongdoing, for when my mother brushed my hair after my nap it fell out in huge clumps, panicking her. Then she saw the bits of Scotch tape I'd used to patch it back on. The jig was up.

Not long afterwards came Spoolies curlers—soft vinyl spools with a large and a smaller end. These worked on the same principle as the rags, but instead of tying a knot, you'd secure them by snapping the large end over the small. They were marginally softer than rags with a bit more boing to them, and ostensibly easier to sleep on, but I wasn't sold.

Was it that other Midwestern girl, Dorothy Gale, who prompted Mom to French-braid my hair every day for a while there? I could barely tolerate the procedure, not because she was rough—she had a gentle ladylike touch—but because sitting still for practically *hours* was so *boring* when you wanted to be outside and moving.

After we both lost patience with the braids, school pictures show me looking less like Dorothy and more like Toto, thanks to awkward tousled haircuts whacked by Mom's stylist. Mom stopped caring.

But around sixth grade, Mom makes a glorious exception. She decides to give me a Toni home permanent. (Its piercing, intoxicating, chemical scent is lodged fondly in olfactory memory next to the gorgeously dizzying fragrance of fresh mimeograph.)

Our kitchen's the only space large enough to accommodate the paraphernalia: mysterious bottles, special purple tissues, three sizes of plastic curling rods, rat-tail comb, cotton balls, raggedy towels (always in rich supply).

I perch on the metal step stool. Mom ties a cape of plastic tablecloth around my neck, then begins the time-consuming process of rolling in each rod. She then surrounds my scalp with a long snake of rolled cotton along my hairline to protect my face and neck and dabs on the perm solution. I feel cold drips on my neck: the Morse code of beauty. She sets the kitchen timer, and when it rings, rinses my head in the sink and applies neutralizer. When I'm dry, voila! Sausagey bangs and tight blond coils in my school picture attest she left it in too long, but my face is beaming with the joy of my mother's attention.

CLOTHING

Mom wore housecoats and robes around the house, but she loved dressing up. Though thick-middled in later years, she had shapely legs and good ankles. She loved a linen sheath with a matching coat. The bitey foxes from Aunt Irene. Chiffon. That black crepe number Dad brought from Paris. Luncheon dressing. Wristwatch a quarter-inch wide. Beige pearls. Black cashmere coat, black cashmere sweater. Good shopper. Taught quality.

Clip-on earrings—the thought of piercing her ears made her blood run cold. Weekly trip to the beauty parlor where they dyed and puffed her hair into a cocoa soufflé, which stained her pillowcase till she got the satin one.

As for me, uniforms were a boring blessing. Same thing every day, but a relief not to guess or think. Essentially democratic.

Navy blue jumpers. Later, blackwatch plaid and red bow ties. In high school, brown wool plaid, dark brown blazers, saddle shoes umber and burnt orange. No matter the uniform, though, the compulsory white blouse.

Unfortunately, laundry, like all housework, held no interest for Mom. Our basement was just shy of gothic and we dreaded it. Crickets and spiders jumped from every corner, like some haunting throwback to Gophertown.

"Laundry" meant dirty smelly clothes, the stinking heap under the chute piling from the cobwebbed laundry room, with clumps of rotting lint in the gray cement sink, all the way up the chute to the first and sometimes second floor; it meant pawing through that reeking pile to find my least dirty school blouse, though the boys' fresh-pressed cadet shirts hung next to Dad's crisp ones—they got done. The boys would get demerits for looking sloppy. I only got *social* demerits.

Not long after my home perm, Mom gave up on my appearance altogether.

I am piling on pounds. Shopping in the chubby section depresses us both. Ladies are not fat, nor are their daughters.

Kako doesn't have to look like anything. She gives Mom spiritual pride. Her two older boys are handsome. Skip is overweight and wears those blocky black glasses, but he's a genius. Jim's cute and so's Ro. But I stick out like the sore thumb I am. I embarrass Mom and she resents it. It will be some time before I learn to be embarrassed by *her*, longer still before I'll actually taste my own resentment tucked into the Twinkie.

She's clearly relieved when I start shopping on my own and sew the occasional article for myself. I love fabric, as I love blank paper, modeling clay, craft items—anything that can become something else. As I myself wish to do.

The Cart

The cart was a double-decker round red metal number we wheeled in and out of the kitchen, conveying stacks of aluminum tumblers, melamine plates, heavy bowls of potato salad, and cold cuts out to the screened porch, or trundling iceberg, wan tomatoes, and "fried" chicken (which Mom shook in a paper bag with seasoned flour and baked before "Shake and Bake" was a gleam in Kraft's eye) over the bumpy carpet into the sunroom for a Sunday dinner watching Walter Cronkite on The Twentieth Century.

This workhorse was swung around by two or three children with one or two riders from time to time, though I swore not to tell. The cart's real moment of glory was rolling the Thanksgiving Turkey to the watering mouths in the dining room.

After years of use, though, it looked like a beat-up old truck—chipped, scratched, and badly in need of a coat of paint.

I would occasionally take such matters into my own hands. I couldn't repair a shower, but I could refinish a table. Browsing at Costello's hardware, paging through wallpaper books, handling tools, and smelling fresh paint afforded joy not far from that of baking. To say nothing of the transformative properties of Contact paper.

One thrilling day at Costello's, I see Contact has come out with plastic adhesive squares that mimic the look of tiny ceramic tiles. I buy a few packages, take them home, and stick them up in our dingy half-bath. A thrilling renovation!

•••

It is never pointed out to me that design is best done in stages—work it out on paper, get it the way you want it, and then paint your surface, so I'm a seat-of the-pants gal.

•••

I apply a bright yellow basecoat to cheer up the cart. Then, inspired by Aunt Irene and Uncle Harry's Mexican postcards, I paint a burro pulling a colorful cart of fruits and vegetables. He sports a jaunty sombrero. It's cute and cart-appropriate yet totally dissatisfies me. Don't know what I want, but it isn't this.

I repaint the whole thing white and consider my new blank slate. Pictures float to consciousness. I grab my little cans of red, brown, blue.

Under my hand appear the following objects, swirling around the blank center: a four-inch tube of Cherries in the Snow lipstick, a hand mirror, a fluffy powder puff, a brimming atomizer, and a pair of red high heels. That's more like it.

Then, right in the middle, I paint the *pièce de résistance*: a waltzing couple, she in dreamy blue dress and bright red lips, he in brown suit and dashing brown pompadour. Oh, how graceful they are! How happy waltzing in each other's arms, emitting little musical notes. Yes, this will do nicely indeed.

•••

While we have our scars and struggles, such a thing was tolerated in our house. No one ever said what's your adolescent fantasy doing on our kitchen cart? Repaint that! If my parents winced at the naked vulnerability shown by their budding chubby daughter, they were kind enough not to say anything. In fact, nobody made anything of it. It just kept making those trips to the screen porch, the sunroom, the dining room table, the waltzing couple warming the turkey from below.

Very Personally Yours

While I'd seen them before—as Mom nursed Ro, or accidentally coming into the bedroom when she was strapping on her bra—and I know something is going on beneath the tight-fitting plaid shirtwaists Timmy's Mom wears on *Lassie*, I never take serious notice of breasts. A shirtwaist or magician's-assistant or Tinkerbelle shape is not in my future. Not with my body, it isn't.

I'm not like anyone on TV or in the movies. Guess I'm not as true. My awareness is sharpened at sleepaway camp.

•••

I like Girl Scouts, the outdoorsiness, the thing-makingness, the information.

Also with a different kind of mother attached. Mrs. Long, our leader, with high-color sweetfeature face, her firm yellow pageboy, lets me read poetry to our troop, and helps me get all these badges, like cooking, art, and first aid. Plus, an adult around, girls aren't so mean.

But at camp, there don't seem to be adults, just kids—high school kids and college kids and us.

Dopey crafts. Stitch two vinyl squares with yarn, stuff with issues of Look and Life, sew it shut for a "sit-upon" at the campfire. Heavy, smelly thing doesn't belong in the woods.

Then pick long grasses for stupid octopus. They give us balls of Styrofoam to drape grasses over and yarn to tie under grassdraped ball for head.

Divvy up grasses, braid into legs. Tie with more yarn, press plastic black-and-white jiggle eyes in.

This stupid thing I'm trying to make this stupid thing here in my bunk while they're over there talking about their boyfriends and their sprouting breasts and I don't have any and I don't want to hear that hers are like apples while hers are pearshape, and here comes their pubic hair, me as bare as a brown'n'serve roll. Stop talking about all this and laughing at me because I don't have any, running from the cabin down a grassy bank clutching my octopus weeping on its braidy legs beating its styrofoam head on a stone over and over.

• • •

I can't talk this over with Mom. Thanks to her upbringing, she is loath to discuss any physical function.

The O'Briens never use the toilet. We "go to the bathroom." We don't pee. If forced to elaborate, we "go Number One or Two." "Belly" is vulgar, only used in accurate but reluctant reference to a stomach-first flop into lake water. "Tummy" is what aches with hunger or indulgence. (Or the flu, which went round the house so often in my earliest days that I thought a stomach was a platform on a spring. The food you ate collected on it and pressed it down till...*boing*.)

I never heard the word "fart" until our racy, grubby neighbor girl Margy (pronounced with a hard g, as in gross, which she loved to be) tells us there's a special name for that "burp at the other end." Of course she refers to butts, which we do not possess. Nor fannies. "Rear end" is tolerable, "behind," preferable. Po-Po is acceptable for the Littles, thanks to the occasional round of that deathless '50s tune: "Feet up, pat him on the po-po / Let's hear him laugh Ha-ha!" When Dad is so angry (not pissed, of course) that he actually uses the word "rump," as in "Get off your rumps and help your mother!" we know we are in big trouble.

So I know a whole lotta nothin' when Dad drops Mom and me off at school that compulsory night when all sixth grade girls and their mothers have to come watch The Movie. It's not the birds and the bees— just the birds. The very same studio that brought us Bambi and Snow White brings us these dreamy-eyed girls and elegant fallopian tubes featured in *The Story of Menstruation*. As the opening credits roll, I am shocked to discover that the word Menstruation has a U in it.

My mother, in her haste to stop talking about it, vocally compresses it to "menstration," which I think is some variant on "adminstration."

(In some sense, I suppose it is.) After the movie, each of us receives a "Very Personally Yours" booklet, a reference I am happy to have, because Mom will be mum.

Eventually these two spoolies start bumping out on my chest. Not like Timmy's mom at all, just two more blobs on an already blobby body, pink knobs notwithstanding (so to speak). But they earn me an undershirt and "training" bra (training of whom for what? training of what for whom?) so that I'll be less embarrassed by my lack of development when we change for gym.

•••

At last, a few years later: "Dear diary, Guess who started what today? Yep, I started. Mom says I should mark off the days in here." I don't. The rest of the entry is about "Ugh!" upcoming semester tests, losing three pounds, and dyeing that beige purse of mine a cool shade of teak brown. Just the important news, folks.

So I learn how to climb into the complex rigmarole of early sixties womanhood.

Sanitary napkins is a misnomer. "Modess" is closer to the junior "mattress" you wear between your legs, just as uncomfortable as it sounds, to say nothing of the weird elastic belt and the oddball front-and-back hooking of it. And in the days before pantyhose, the dressier occasions that call for nylons mean you wear a garter belt to hold them up. All this engineering under your skirt fosters twisting, binding, and wedging at every opportunity. Chubby Checker causes pleasure and discomfort in equal measure.

Tampons do exist. Their ads feature "gals in white pants." But Mom frowns at the very idea. A girl shouldn't put anything "in there." Discomfort aside, that's okay. At my weight I'm never going to wear white pants.

But I insist on shaving my legs. Mom tries to talk me out of it. "Leave it the way it is. It's light. If you shave now, you'll have to shave forever."

"I can't wear nylons with leg hair pressing under them! I don't want to be a hairy monster. The other girls will make fun of me."

I cannot get a razor fast enough. I have enough strikes against me.

•••

Of course neither movie nor booklet nor Mom offers any clue as to how a graceful little egg gets "impregnated" and sets up shop in the "somewhat velvety" uterus. How the heck is "the miracle of life" actually passed on?

Ro and I have shared many a hoot over this.

"We were so sheltered," she says. "At twelve I knew nothing. How did you find out?"

"I knew better than to ask Mom and Dad. I scoured the dictionary. 'Sex' was no help, or 'genitals' or 'man' or 'woman.' But when I finally looked up 'male' and 'female' and found the reference to electric plugs, I put two and two together, so to speak. I later fine-tuned it by snagging *The Facts of Life and Love for Teenagers* at the Bookmobile. Double sin. Reading about sex was bad enough, but I wasn't even a teenager. Thank God for compassionate librarians."

How we laugh.

"At least we got a little head start," says Ro. "Mom didn't know a thing until the night before she married Dad. Aunt Irene gave her a 'submit unto thy husband' lecture."

"Can you imagine? They couldn't talk about any of it. Ever, it seemed. When I was thirteen, I found a racy paperback in the attic— some Hollywood pulp. I took it to my room and was stunned that a book could have such an effect on my body. 'Course, I didn't know how noisy I was."

"Oh, no—Mom?"

"Worse. Dad. Opens the door. 'What's going on in here?' I was dumbstruck. 'Did you have the pillow between your legs?' he asks. I'm absolutely mortified. 'Yes.' 'Aw, honey,' he says, in the saddest, most reproachful tone. 'Leave sex to the married people.' That was it. No further illumination, instruction. God, it was awful. I don't think I could look at him for a week."

Ro, ever practical, says, "What I want to know is who bought that racy book?"

Not Normal

In seventh grade, I really start to wonder what's wrong with me. I need help. I pick up the phone.

"Hello, Betsey? It's Reenie."

"Who?" Darn. Why can't I have a nickname?

"Irene. Sometimes we walk to school?"

"Huh?"

"Or, I mean, I catch up to you?"

"Oh, sure. Hi."

"I'm calling because..." Throat closing off. *I'm not going to cry, don't cry, she'll help you, she's nice. She's not fat but she won't make fun. You're both the same, smart.* "Because if I had to be marooned on a desert island, you'd be the friend I'd choose."

Silence. Her parakeet chitters and squawks.

"Um, so I wondered...I wanted to ask you..."

Her silence gets silenter.

Gush of teary fear and need: "I have to know. I try to be nice and funny and have good heart. Why don't people like me and be my friend?"

"Oh." Relief. Then awkwardly, kindly: "Maybe if you do something about your appearance? Maybe launder your blouses more?'

"I'm messy. So that's it?" Relief. Laundry. I'm glad she can't see that I'm talking on the wall phone in our shameful crickety spidery basement, smelling the unwashed clothing from here.

"Gosh. Well. Thanks. I will. See you at school."

Appearances aren't supposed to count, what counts is inside. But I begin to wash and press with urgency. Press out the awkwardness, the fat, press friendship in.

But it doesn't seem to take.

A few months later, per Mom's request, I'm vacuuming my parent's bedroom. The only sound louder and more unpleasant than the harsh abrasion of the motor is my inner monologue.

Thought Jane was my friend but she turned against me even though I try to keep my blouses clean now, but homework's more important because you don't get a grade on your blouse.

Scrape. Shove the upright over the nubby carpet.

But she had me over but now she's busy, but why? What's wrong with me?

Who can I talk to only my cousin Katy who I only ever see two weeks in summer. What's wrong with me? I'm not normal.

Tears blister down.

Mom comes in for her paperback.

"Don't forget to vac the bath mat this week," she says.

I start crying in earnest.

"I'm not normal!"

"Oh for heaven's sake. Of course you are."

"I am not! I don't have any friends and size twenty-two and a half is NOT NORMAL!"

"Don't say that. You're normal."

I can't believe Mom won't admit it.

"LOOK at me. You can see I'm not normal! I'm NOT NORMAL!" Sobbing, sobbing like a toddler.

"If you don't stop crying, I'll do what I did when you were little. I'll throw cold water in your face."

"You wouldn't dare."

She leaves me blubbering, clutching the upright vacuum.

She returns with a blue aluminum tumbler of cold water and throws it in my face.

Icy rivulets. Cold is cold.

Exposure

A landscape is a thing you find yourself in. It's hardly a thing you're aware you have entered until it gets dramatic.

We walk landscapes on maps: the body's whole topography limned on the soles of our feet. Trunk lines meet in these elegant structures supporting it all.

I have one foot in the warmth of Dad's world and one in the arctic of Mom's.

Continued exposure in glacial conditions leads to a loss of sensation. Toes and arch and ankle numb, then freeze. Extended exposure blackens, then detaches them.

If only I think a certain way, my foot will be there. If I change my behavior, if I am a really good person, my foot will come back. If I strap this brick in its place I won't even notice. If I chop the other one off I might regain my balance.

Oh, void. Oh, foot I do not have. Oh, elaborate contraption I build to propel myself.

The Living Water

Maybe I'm not praying enough.

I decide to aim for the highest award a Catholic Girl Scout can achieve: The Marian Award. It entails a yearlong study of the Blessed Virgin, acquiring knowledge of Church liturgy, vestments, and objects, completing a public service project, and writing an essay. For good spiritual and physical discipline, I also try losing weight at the same time with Metrecal and Ayds.

I flop at weight loss, but continue my study of the Ideal Mother: God's Own. When I earn my Marian Medal, everyone's proud of me, me included. Even Mom.

The Church was living water flowing through our landscape, with weekly waterings at Mass, rosaries recited in the car or doing dishes, bent-knee Lenten mornings, waterfalling into the great cyclical feasts marked in our home by the lotiony scent of lilies or the prickle of the Advent Wreath. High ecclesiastical tide culminated in our personal rites of Catholic passage: First Communion and Confirmation, conferring the sense of blessed, sanctioned growth.

In our early years, security bloomed because of The Living Water: the weekly rhythm of Mass; the strange comfort of Latin, like a grunting affectionate animal; the soaring healing music—not just organs full of Bach and Mozart, but many lesser melodic mortals—laying down hymns like blocks of stone, simplicity and certainty in every note. Chest-resonant, this joy of choir harmony both heard and sung—voices enter the body like scent.

The Church fostered appreciation of the arts beyond sweet Breck-hair Jesus pointing at his glowing heart or Mary weeping at his twisted torso on the crucifix. We gaze at sculpted Stations of the Cross, brilliances of stained glass, intricacy and beauty of embroidered vestments. We hear poetry of Psalms and parables, the drama of the Gospels. Enjoy the theatricality of a good sermon, which we review as pointedly as Times critics. The mysterious beauty of words on the parish-issued calendar: Liturgical Year. Ember Days. Ordinary Time.

Welcome, too, the constantly refreshing idea that you could be forgiven on the spot if you were sorry enough and did your penance. The sense of belonging to a larger entity nourishes the spirit. The belief in the non-physical aspects of ourselves. The gravitas of tradition.

To say nothing of seeing your own Dad at Midnight Mass on Christmas Eve looking like an ambassador in a throne room when he wears the full magnificent Knights of Columbus regalia: sweeping red-lined black cape, sash and sword, black velvet chapeau brimming with a snowy ostrich plume.

The Church. On the one hand, great comfort. But in the palm of the other hand, the oozing wound: "You're born bad, you can't be trusted, and you must do what we say."

Flowing through the desert of self-doubt, The Living Water gets saltier and saltier over the years, evaporating, condensing to a lump of salt. Immobile. Causing, no longer quenching, thirst.

Like Bedouins, we're forced to lick the dew which collects on stones at sunrise.

Montana, Day Five: Beach Eats

Does the wilderness forgive? Certainly the people here do.

And for those brought up to search outside for confirmation, wilderness is the ultimate outside in which to search. Here, survival itself is confirmation.

•••

No one knows that better than Jim.

How I admire my little brother, who can steer a raft, manage a saddlehorse, guide a son. Let me correct that. Jim'll offer advice, but lets his boys choose for themselves. He once risked death for this principle.

•••

He and the boys are on horseback out in The Bob, and Mike is old enough to be Trail Boss for the first time. All decisions are his to make.

"Let's take a shortcut up this hiking trail."

"Sure you want to do that, son? Horses don't belong on hiking trails."

"Trail looks solid, Dad. It'll cut a mile off our trip."

"You're The Boss."

But hiking trails are softer, differently maintained. Jim's horse rounds a bend and loses its footing, and Mike watches in horror as man and horse disappear off a steep bank of scree.

"I've killed my Dad! I've killed my Dad!"

Jim's here to tell this story because he had learned how to throw himself off a falling horse. Neither he or the horse suffered anything serious.

Letting people make their own mistakes is what takes real courage.

Since the day they let you keep your fingers, Jim, you've endured lifetimes worth of medical and emotional anguish in yourself and those you love and you still come up smelling like charcoal-grilled steak.

You're sustained by a faith you say you feel unworthy to nurture.
(How can that be?) You love the deep old Latin Church, you love good
talk, you love your sons beyond life itself, and are as beautifully distilled
a spirit as any you like to sip.

•••

Sister, brother, nephews, niece. It's so beautiful to be with them all.
The music of their presence drowns out any words I could use for them.
I'm swept in spinning rapids of emotion.

That night, at Derek's suggestion, we haul dinner down to the
beach. Mike grills glazed pork skewers, with eggplant for vegetarian Ro.
Tasty, relaxing, refreshing.

Don has also brought a full-size six-liter gravity water filter. We fill
it with river water and hang that heavy sucker from a tree.

I offer to do the dishes, scrubbing off the worst in a pan of warm
soapy water, then rinsing with filtered water.

Washing dishes at the water's edge is a very pure, ancient feeling.

Then I regard my little squeeze bottle. By day two, my camp soap
has been so generously used by other dishwashers that there's nearly
none left for my other proud applications: hair, shower, clothing. I want
to hide it like some character on *Twilight Zone*. Or some kid who grew
up in a big family.

It has yet to dawn on me there will be no hair washing or
showering. If they didn't pack first aid, you can bet there's no camp
shower. Clothing? Ridiculous to wash—I'm constantly wet on the river.

•••

I carry back the dripping dishes to dry by the fire and pull out the
Mad-Libs "Literature" pad. A glorious hilarious game ensues. Peter
Pan and Alice in Wonderland repopulated with silly nouns and verbs—
stories even the young'uns scream with laughter over. The very best of
the old Tangletown dinner table.

As the game winds down, we hear a coarse, peculiar
sound. Close by.

Shocking, the rapid shift from laughter to fear, like yesterday's
rapid shifts from shifting rapids and pounding heart to the stately blue
flow, absent of human touch, wire, litter, metal, paper, plastic—a world
all green, all flight, all needle and leaf and brush and cloud—which
swiftly shifts again to threat.

Hearts pounding, we secure bear spray and flashlights.

Creating My Own Reality

Summer between eighth grade and high school I make a firm, intuitive decision. *I just won't be shy anymore. That's all there is to it. Hardly anyone at my new Catholic girls' high school will know me, and those who do won't care.*

"How To Win Friends and Influence People" from the Bookmobile is the answer to my prayers. I'll shower the attention I have not received: Friend to All, Friend to the Misfit, Friend to The Different.

Passing in the halls between classes—that Times Square of High School—I greet everyone, even those I know from grade school. Coining nicknames, magnanimous, driving my personality through the halls like a brand-new '65 Pontiac.

Get involved. Like a maple tree loosing helicopters, fluttering bits of myself all over the school. Clean up? I'm there. Chorus? I'm in. Plan the St. Patrick's Assembly? You betcha.

At last I meet My Best Friend.

February 1966. Batman flooding the airwaves. Freshmen always stage the St. Patrick's Assembly. "What about Patman and Robin?" I say. The Committee laughs. Acceptance. "He could fight 'Big Orange.' "

(What are the Irish? What is TV?)

Suddenly someone with blue eyes, a scotch complexion, very long shiny brown hair makes suggestions back at me. "What if—then we could—then Patman says—"

Two musicians jamming for the first time.

"That's right, Robin. Big Orange will be on ice a long time in the cooler!"

A gymnasium of groans and laughter. A hit!

And a person I'm 'specially glad to greet in the halls.

The year opens into spring, then summer. Doing dishes one night I hear her name on the radio. She's sent the DJ a suggestion. I can't believe it. I call her.

She hadn't been listening. We talk a long time.

•••

She goes on a trip and she sends me a postcard. I never got one from anyone not a relative. Would I like to be in the Jan and Dean fan club? Sure would!

We stay in touch over the summer. *She* actually calls *me*. The first day of school we seek each other out, begin a conversation lasting fifteen years.

Sleepovers are best. We don't have to stop talking. Doritos and malted milk balls, Judy Collins. We sleep at her house more than mine.

It's amazing learning someone else's landscape.

Her house has a sense of intention ours lacks. A small house—two parents, two kids (younger brother)—but well-thought-out.

Objects have places. Things in our house just land somewhere. They have a teal blue and lime green color scheme. We have no scheme at all. Their pillows are wooly and woven, not smelly and bunched-up. We have a painting of John-John saluting the casket. They have framed sheet music and a funny Peanuts calendar. Such a cool planter! Looks like a Frisco townhouse. Wit, texture, sophistication. Piles of *New Yorkers*. (Her Dad taught journalism at the University.) And fittingly, her mother's framed collection of barbed wire.

For all her taste, I remember her mother's tart tongue, my deep-set feeling that she didn't like me.

And I felt the chill in that marriage like an open freezer door. Her parents lived side by side like neighbors hardly speaking except to argue about whose apples fell on whose side of the fence and lay there rotting and who had to clean them up and "it's not even my tree."

At least there's warmth between my parents.

•••

Now I'm making friends because I'm being a friend and now I'm being in plays because my best friend can drive and get us there and

I get to be in *All My Sons* and say, "I resent living next door to the Holy Family!"

And we sing and write scripts together and I make more real friends. They laugh at my jokes. One of them smokes and two of them drink and two of them want to kill themselves, but I help talk them out of it.

(I don't smoke or drink—I want my gold watch—but I do press a razorblade into my wrist once just deep enough to know I didn't want to do it.)

•••

Of course I'm still fat. I'm overeating and in our house we don't have bodies. Since childhood I'd been carefully carrying nitroglycerin pills in their little brown bottle downstairs, pills that Dad took for his mending heart, pills I was scared I would drop and blow our landscape all to smithereens. Dad's "bad" heart kept him from the sports he'd loved, or even marching in The Rosary Parade (for which I would have given many things to be a bead). Dad can't swim with you, can't play ball. Dad cannot be physical at all. And so we learn to place the head and heart above the body's grace.

•••

But one night he risks it all: The Daddy-Daughter Dinner Dance.

He cancels a professional engagement to go with me that night. We talk and joke, as always, and dance the slower tunes, but a wild polka tempo comes up.

"A schottische!" he cries. "Well, I'm game!" It was the most and fastest you had ever moved in all my life, that single dance, and we whirled and whirled around the world, blue and white streamers fluttered from the basketball hoops and the foil stars swung.

•••

Later on, he says, "If you ever get in trouble, come to me."

"Thanks," I say, clueless. What's he talking about? I'll never get in trouble. I'll never disappoint you. The love the love the love the love the almost unbearable love.

Renovation

"Why don't we give a luncheon for your friends?"

A luncheon in the Sixties—horrifying thought.

"Mom, nobody does that anymore! Everyone would laugh at me."

Later with my friends, I laugh at her. "She's so out of it. She never asks what I want, what I feel. It's all how it reflects *her*."

How do you prove who you are to someone who will not see you?

•••

My scorn of her offerings is exceeded only by her contempt of mine.

The summer I return from my first painful work-study scholarship year at the teeny girl's college in Madison, Mom and Dad take two weeks in Scottsdale, Arizona, their first private vacation in decades.

A few mornings after they leave, I go to the kitchen, reach for a glass.

Our ever-dirty cupboards. Wouldn't Mom be tickled if I cleaned them?

I throw away the ancient mayo jars, the crusting ketchup, the rusting cocoa tin, replace the cruddy newsprint with fresh Delft-pattern shelf paper, and step back to admire my sparkling shelves.

But the cupboard doors are streaky with years of grease and cigarette smoke, your smoke, your hypnotizing smoke that slowed you into stories over the black kitchen table.

I see with fresh eyes, eyes that for two semesters have been elsewhere.

What does it mean—this kitchen? What do these colors mean— these supposedly white walls? Who called for these chrome-edged shrill-red Formica countertops? These gray plastic tiles? Whose idea was this chewy blue and white linoleum? This table, this oval abyss of black metal, reflecting chomping jaws, clattering flatware?

Who found these awful coffee-potted curtains—which actually combine this unappetizing color scheme: red, black, gray, and white? All of it lit by ghostly bouncing blue fluorescent light?

"It looked modern once," you said. "Sophisticated."

This meant, I guess, a place for people who drank martinis to mix them.

Yet you despised it, too. "Someday I'll get a new kitchen."

•••

After I wash the cupboards, the dingy walls cringe.

I'd read your *Family Circles*. I could—what the heck?—repaint those walls and cupboards with a nice glossy enamel. Costello's, here I come.

But when cupboards and the walls are spanking white, the sad scratched linoleum looks like a kennel floor.

Those ads for simple self-stick floors—I have my tuition fund from waitressing, don't I? When will I get another chance to give a gift this big?

I drive to Sears and buy a brand-new kitchen floor, cut and fit and lay the shiny no-wax tiles all Saturday and Sunday.

The kitchen looks like a glittering showroom. You'll be so happy.

Except of course, the gray plastic tiles on the windowless wall look like pigeon filth.

More than paint is called for. More than Contact paper mimicking ceramic tiles. Sears has wood paneling—*genuine* wood—stained a rich walnut. Back to my fund, back to the store, back to the house, panels roped to the car-top.

I measure the panels and cut them with a handsaw.

Whatever certitude of love or of design buoyed me through the washing of the shelves, the painting of the cabinets, the transformation of my lifelong kitchen floor, utterly abandons me when, crowbar in hand, I face the gray plastic tiles.

The root of my tongue pulses. My fingers tingle. I could wait till you get back. We could panel it together, or take it back because what if you don't like it but of course you will. You'll *love* it. You've been wishing for this kitchen all our lives. I *must* do it now. I'll never have another chance—school will start, I won't have time; the panels will prop against the wall and never get installed.

And what good is Cinderella in a golden gown if the coach is still a pumpkin? The transformation has to be complete. *Step into my beautiful room made for you, made of love. Let me fulfill your dream.*

There was something fierce about it, too. Stop talking about a new kitchen and *do it.*

I swing the crowbar, shattering the plastic tiles.

I'm up all night cutting, fitting, nailing, but am too exhausted to apply the trim along the very top.

When Mom and Dad come up the walk, I catapult to meet them.

"I have a big surprise for you!" I squeak in glee and lead them to the new kitchen, clean kitchen, bright kitchen, kitchen of love and warm wood.

You stiffen at the threshold.

"Come in, come in…" I spin around. "Do you like it? I did it mostly myself, though Jim and Ro helped with the floor."

"What a surprise." You resist entering. As if contagion awaits.

"You always said you wanted a new kitchen. Now you have it. What do you think?"

Your gaze swivels corner to corner.

"I'm very surprised."

"That's genuine wood paneling. Not fake. I used my tuition money, but I can waitress more this summer."

Your silence expands, extends and coats the room, settles like dust on wet paint. Finally it sinks into me, smothering my lungs.

Your old prescription: If you can't say something nice, don't say anything at all.

My heart is punching. You can't say something nice. Not one nice thing? Not even "A for effort"? I want to scream, to sob, but I won't give you the satisfaction.

In continued silence, without so much as an awkward smile, you go upstairs to unpack, guillotining any further outreach.

But magnified through my suspended tears, I see the admiration in Dad's eyes.

He puts his arm around my shoulder.

"Congratulations, Honey. This is just remarkable, what you've done."

"Thanks, Dad." The floodgates open. "I thought she'd like it. I'm sorry if I did something wrong. She just always said she wanted—"

"I'm proud of you, Honey. It was very generous of you, but you shouldn't have used your tuition money. I'm going to reimburse you."

"It was gonna be my gift—"

He gives me his handkerchief. "That's all right; I'll take care of it."

When it came, I took the money. The trim went unattached for years.

•••

Memory is curious.

The first night of our Montana trip, when Jim and Ro and I were sharing that sunset drink on the deck, talking family, Jim asked, "Did you think Mom treated you any worse than she treated the rest of us?"

"No, not really," I confessed.

"I'm here to tell you she did. She *did* treat you worse. You got her goat. She didn't like you. I remember she slapped you once."

"Slapped me? Really? I don't remember."

"Yes, she did. I remember that," Ro corroborates. Neither remembers why.

The icy water still drips down my face, my lungs still suffocate about the kitchen, but the slap is deeply buried, like uranium.

"Wow," I said. "And she thought saying 'belly' was rude."

Thank God a sense of humor was valued in our house.

Motherland

When a volcano meets a glacier and it will not melt, which retreats?

In early years, eruptions blasted from my core. By this time, fury's burning underground in lava lakes and lava rivers. I won't know it's there for years.

Lava seeks its level. When it surfaces, it rigidifies as it cools. All I feel is hurt and grief. I have no idea I'm angry. I just eat and hate myself and eat.

•••

In their long, slow inching over landscapes, glaciers rake terrain, pluck out boulders, leave holes gaping in the land. This is their nature.

They also create a blue beauty; fascinating for what's caught inside. Their broken places don't absorb light, but reflect, refract, bend it, throwing it back at the viewer. Some people, when love strikes their broken places, bend and throw it back as well.

What's caught in Mom is early breakage.

•••

Let me go all the way back to you, Betty, at four, in Omaha, holding the hand of an unseen someone. You wear bows the size of Easter baskets on your head and a quizzical pout. This photograph is not casual. It was something to remember you by.

Your mother Grace is folding laundry, pairing little stockings, placing them in a basket, speaking with her younger sister.

"It's wonderful how you get Betty to sleep, Irene."

"She loves anything that rhymes." Irene smoothes a little dress. "Pretty little frock."

"I don't have your ease with her. She will miss you terribly."

"How can you think of leaving Omaha, Grace?"

"It's John. He wants a new start."

"But Mother's not herself. It would kill her if you go. And should Betty travel when she's not thriving? Harry thinks it's her kidneys."

"He told us. We're blessed to have a pediatrician in the family. But John wants to live in Los Angeles."

"Oh, Grace, that awful place? Bring up a child in that moral turpitude? Omaha is so civilized. We have real society now. Our dazzling new Hotel Fontenelle and its cultural events—"

"John won't stay in Omaha another minute. We have just enough money to get to California."

"Don't be silly. Stay with *us*. Mother *loves* Betty. So do we."

Grace sits next to Irene.

"That's what I wanted to talk to you about, Sister. We don't want to live off you or Mother, but since Betty's unwell, we thought the best place for her—that is, until she's better—would be with you and Harry. We'll get settled in California and send for her. "

"Grace, you can't mean that. Why not just stay until she's well?"

"John's lawsuit failed. The Creightons won't pay what they owed his mother."

"I don't understand."

"When they sold the family farm, her brothers used the proceeds to build the Pacific Telegraph line. Promised their sister they'd settle up with her. They made a fortune, and she never saw a dime. When her last brother died, John should have received her share, but the court ruled against him."

"That's terrible. But surely there's work *here*?"

"He can't watch Creighton College being built with his inheritance.

"You'd leave your child behind?"

"I'd leave my child with you, which isn't quite behind. We'll save up money and send for her when Betty's healthy."

"Grace, how can you leave your *firstborn child*?!"

"With my sister who *longs* for a child. With a doctor who can make her well. With my mother, who is happier and sharper whenever she's around. Please say yes, Irene. It's best for everyone."

Grace holds out the basket of Betty's clothing. With a quaking hand Irene accepts it. Her dearest wish has just come true.

•••

That photograph of you was literally a parting shot, the image for your parents to remember you by. Years passed and Grace and John never sent for you. They led a new life in California, had three more children, and never sent for you.

There is speculation they made the request but that Aunt Irene and Uncle Harry didn't want to give you back. They loved you as their own. You were growing up with social advantages. No one wanted to cast Betty's grandmother into despair. You stayed with her during the week and Aunt Irene and Uncle Harry on the weekends.

Never spoken, the obvious truth: parents who truly wanted their child would have retrieved her.

All of them lavished attention on you, which earned you your nickname, "Queenie." Here you are at nine, cavorting for the camera, devising entertainments, veils of Araby, a wreath of laurel 'round your brow for recitation.

Forsaken by your parents, robbed of your siblings, primal abandonment cracked your first blue unsealable fissure. Though your relatives meant well, their excessive praise (and sometimes excessive criticism) as well as their overindulgence could not fill that fissure. Instead, they unwittingly helped form your abscess of narcissism, which seeped throughout our childhood.

At Gobby's Knee

You always wanted to write a book about your grandmother and call it *The Valiant Woman*. "Grandmother" too big for your child mouth, you called her Gobby.

Gobby towered. A formidable widow with a huge hive of hair and suspicion in her eye, she brought you up an only child in a manless house, double-mothered by Aunt Irene on Saturdays, with Uncle Harry for a dad once a week.

You never wrote a word of your book, though. The details below are all we know.

•••

Gobby unpins her immense head of hair. Though it's 1923, she persists in wearing the 1890s Gibson Girl.

"Can I sit on your lap while you brush your hair?"

"The question is 'May I?" and the answer is no. A lady doesn't do that."

So Betty perches at her knee.

"*One. Two.* Remember, child, a hundred brush strokes every night. *Three.* A woman's hair is her crowning glory."

"I know, Gobby. I did mine already. Tell me about when you were little. Was there candy in those days?"

"Yes, you little sugar-fiend. I got five pennies of my own each week and parceled them out. *Eleven.* Bought one stick of candy every day. *Twelve.* Be sure you brush all the way to the end."

"What else?"

"I had a red pom-pom hat with a flippy tassel that I loved, but I never had any more curls than you and I wanted them ten times more. *Eighteen.* I'd wet my hair and wrap it around a stick."

"A stick? How silly."

"Don't be impertinent. On important occasions, I'd borrow two curls and drape them over my bosom."

"Did your mother and father leave you behind, too?"

"Don't lean into me, child. It's rude. Bodies were not made for touching. *Twenty-six.* My parents could afford to keep me."

"What did your Papa do?"

"After they came from Ireland to Joliet in 1835, Papa worked on the Canal and Mama helped women have babies. *Thirty-one.* They did well. Not every young lady is privileged to attend St. Mary's College in South Bend."

"Did you like it?"

"I reveled in my English classes. But the Sisters insisted on sewing hour, which I hated. *Thirty-seven.* I struck a bargain with the other girls. They did my mending while I told them stories."

"Did you have many suitors?"

"I had my share. I was once engaged to a candy store owner. *Forty-three.* But I did so love my name. Ellen Langdon. People thought I was crazy, but I swore I'd never change it, even when I married. Where was I?"

"How'd you meet Judge?"

"*Fifty.* Joliet, Illinois, was 'tedious as a twice-told tale,' as Shakespeare would say. I wanted to live. So I decided to move to California."

"Just like Mother and Father."

"Yes, except I didn't get there. I stopped ten miles from here in Papillion to visit Mama's relatives. *Fifty-five.* They met me in a buckboard and took me to their farm for a spell. That's when I met Mart. He wasn't Judge yet. He was Superintendent of Schools."

"Was he your Prince?"

"Smartest man I ever met. When he was young, he lived in a sod house on the prairie, coldest place you can imagine in the winter. *Sixty-three.* Wind and snow blowing through cracks in the turf."

"Why would you live in the dirt?"

"That's how you laid claim to land. He never went to school till he was fourteen, and in five years he was *teaching* school. *Seventy.* And few years later he was Superintendent of *all* the schools."

"When did he ask you to marry him?"

"Stop squirming. First, he asked me to teach. So many immigrants were coming for jobs on the Transcontinental Railway. It was better than the old country because they could earn their own land. All of them wanted to educate their children.

" 'I can't even draw a straight line with a ruler,' I told him. But The Judge was persuasive even before he became a lawyer. *Seventy-seven.*"

"When did you marry? What did you wear?"

"Sit still. I'm losing count. *Seventy-nine.* April 30, 1878. April because, always remember...?"

" 'The bride of May will fade away.' "

"Good girl. *Eighty-three.* I wore a blue taffeta gown."

"Did you live in a sod house too?"

"No, silly poppet. Mama gave us eighty acres of good farmland as a wedding present. Well, she gave it to me. 'I won't give it to Mart,' she said. 'He'd only buy books with it.'

"It's true. *Eighty-nine.* Mart loved learning and he studied law at night. He passed the bar, opened his practice, and became County Judge. Then we moved here to

Omaha. No more questions, Queenie! You've made me lose count again!

"*Ninety-five,* it's *ninety-five.*"

"Say your prayers and off to bed with you. But first, what stuff are we?"

" 'We are such stuff as dreams are made on, and all our lives are little rounded sleep.' "

" 'Rounded *with* a little sleep.' Now, 'Goodnight, goodnight, a thousand times good night.' "

"Just one more. Did you have to change your name?"

"I never did. The Lord saw to it Mart's last name was Langdon, too. *One hundred.*"

Vigils

Gobby loved the theatre. She and Aunt Irene would go together every Thursday.

"I hated Thursdays," you told us. "There was no one home."

But Gobby came back full of magical tales and acted them out in the dark apartment by lamplight after stew: growling, sweeping, yardstick whacking on the horsehair couch, while you, fair Desdemona, squealed in delicious fear.

Gobby had fears of her own, though. She stayed in bed every Friday the Thirteenth. This was presented as good sense, not fear. Thunder found her under covers, too. She was never at home in the natural world.

Hers was a stern fierce love:

"Gobby, Gobby, I got all As except one B!"

"Why did you get the B?"

But your good grades and veils and leading roles ("I'm cast as the Prince in *The Student Prince*, Gobby!") could not stop her descent into madness.

When you were eleven, a terrifying night left its mark.

•••

Gobby has locked the door of the bedroom she and you share and cannot find the key. She begins to pace.

"The door is locked. The door is locked! What will we do? We'll never get out. What if there's a fire?"

She's circling the tiny room. She's pulling at her snowy braids.

"Oh God have mercy on our souls. We're going to burn to death!"

You study her. Gobby's wringing her hands. It's a theatre quiz.

"You're the lady with the spots, Gobby, right? Who can't wash them out?"

You tug her nightgown.

Gobby's rakes her braids apart and spins in fury. Her thick hair, fallen like a shawl, whips you in the eye. You start to cry.

"I don't know her name. Is it Beth? Lady Beth?"

Gobby grabs your shoulders, shakes your thin frame.

"This is not a game. We can't get out! There's going to be a fire and we're going to burn to death and there's nothing we can do!"

She throws herself against the door and pounds and pounds: a bleeding fist, a blazing face, a hornet's nest of hair.

"Dear God have mercy on our souls!"

She yanks you from the corner, shoves you to your knees.

"We've got to pray. Pray the rosary! Oh, we're going to burn to death! We're going to burn to death tonight! Pray, Queenie, pray! And don't fall asleep!"

All night long as you choke out prayers, Gobby paces, wrings her hands, kneels, crawls, beseeches God, vilifies herself, shakes you when you nod off, "Fire! Fire! We're going to die!"

Somehow in the morning the key is found, or the door swings open, or it was never locked. That was not the part that mattered.

•••

You kept other vigils of madness. As you grew, Gobby diminished. More superstitious, more suspicious, she kept to her bed more days than not.

In seventh grade, you come home to hear Gobby caterwauling:

"You!? Where's Betty? I want Betty!"

"Here I am!" You race to her bedside. "I'm here, Gobby, I'm here!"

An icy fearful gaze.

"No, not you. Betty!"

"But I am Betty!"

"No, I want Betty, not you! Where's Betty?"

•••

How do you prove who you are to someone who will not see you?

To have had a place and see it disappear again.

•••

"It broke my heart," you told us. Abandoned, again abandoned, no way to follow. All you could do was watch identity dissolve, yours as well as Gobby's.

At last Gobby died.

"Live with us now, Darling," Aunt Irene and Uncle Harry said to you, now seventeen. "Stay as long as you like. We so bitterly regret not legally adopting you."

"I was so grateful," you later said. "It allowed me to mourn Gobby and not cry for my own fate."

Not long afterward, you started dating Dad, started college, and became Social Secretary at the Hotel Fontenelle. All dainty napkins and luncheons, seashell soap, scalloped dishes, all that is breakable, linen, or white. None of the Omaha rough stuff, no great outdoors, no salty buckaroo for you.

Montana, Day Five: That Sound

We freeze in our tracks. A neck-prickling sound over too fast to process. A growl?

I want to hear it again to make sense of it, but I don't want to hear it again.

Now I get why the elk femur disturbed me. Elk don't just leave their bones willy-nilly. Somebody ate somebody. And licked their chops and may be hanging out in this happy hunting ground.

The smoke of the skewered pork may have traveled.

We taste like pork, we're told.

"Fan out," says Jim quietly.

We do. Not too far away from each other, armed with (useless) bear spray to protect our area, which, of course, belongs to other animals. It is not really ours at all. Can we still startle wild animals?

Wild is evaporating, wild untouched by humans, that is—which is why, while I hate the fear and discomfort I didn't sign up for, I'm equally honored to witness, participate, breathe and have powerful emotions in what's left of the wilderness.

We hear the word corridors now applied to wilderness. Corridors are the narrow, socially-challenging places we navigated in school, not fit accommodation for the diversity and majesty of wild species. This cellular tragedy fizzes in my bloodstream along with the knowledge *I* don't belong here. But if I am here, perhaps I can speak of it and people will know to preserve it even if they can't stand being there.

We hear it again, with length and clarity this time: an eerie skirling bellow.

"Elk bugle," says Jim. Profound sonic gift. Collective sigh. Collective shoulders dropping. A little trash talk, a few jokes. We wend our way back.

"Too bad Dooley missed this," says Jack. "He would had fun."

"Or been a bear's breakfast," says Mike. "It's too bad Seidlitz missed this."

"We'll tell him tomorrow night," says Jim. "He'll probably beat us to the campsite."

That's right. Seidlitz. Walking in to meet us. Walking us back to his car. Ice-cold beer waiting in his car for us at the trailhead. The end is in sight.

But tomorrow we're back on the water.

"But this part'll be so much easier," says Mike. Jim and Jack agree. They are sensitive, good-hearted men. They've seen our distress. "When we meet up with the White River, the Flathead broadens. Fewer twists and turns. Plenty more water between the banks. Piece of cake."

As I drop off to sleep, though, I wonder why that gut-clutch, that skin-prickle seemed familiar. Our family never camped, we were never near bears.

"Don't be ludicrous! You don't know what you're talking about! What would you even know about fear?" And then of course I realize. That roar is like Skip's voice, internalized.

Rocky Terrain

However wide the landscape, certain elements have stronger impact than others.

Who is stopping me, who is going to pin me to the facts? From whom must I defend my every step? Who's going to tell me my logic is wrong, my facts are screwed, I don't know what I'm talking about? That would be my brother Skip. The dukes I put up at age six stayed up for decades.

Rocky, treacherous place in my landscape: this brother I feared, full of craggy ironies.

He discarded the name Skip in eighth grade and insisted we call him by his birth name, John. John grew up to be a brilliant classical guitarist people sought out for weddings and brunches. Comfort, gentility, precision distinguished his playing, but were absent from most of his conversation.

A peace activist who lay on railroad tracks to stop weapons trains, he often seemed devoid of personal sensitivity or even social skills. Never knowing when to yield the floor, he was a constant filibuster for himself and his opinions, which were mostly dire. Never sensing when he'd hurt your feelings, he'd use his sharp mind like a blunt instrument, to clobber you with facts. (This strategic mind served him well in chess and tournament-level bridge.) The guy could just drive you crazy.

Our best times were always creative. For example, our "radio shows."

In 1965, Tom received his Army officer's commission. He was stationed in Germany. Since overseas long-distance rates cost the equivalent of $86.00 for three minutes, like many families we got a cassette tape recorder to make and listen to audio letters from Tom. Using the recorder, John, Jim, and I invent and enact radio shows We interview Dracula and his daughter, a hyena trainer, Chef Boyardee and other notables, laughing ourselves silly listening to the playbacks.

But better than our "broadcasts," music really brought us together.

In high school, Mom and Dad gave Tom a guitar for Christmas. John couldn't put it down. It absorbed him as nothing ever had. Tom left it to him when he went to college.

By the time John reached high school, he had developed real proficiency. He'd sing and play and I'd harmonize. Together we'd "hoist up the John B sails," "Row the boat ashore," and cover Peter Paul and Mary numbers, Woody Guthrie anthems, whaling songs, and a particularly devastating version of "The Spring Hill Mining Disaster." Bone and blood is the price of coal.

Our piercing harmonies made us both proud. We practiced when we could and performed for the family. Not too often—both of us were in high school with play practice, debate, and all the other extracurriculars. But the speechless communion of song forged a bond that was to surprise me as the tumultuous sixties unfolded in assassinations, riots, and explosive protests against the Viet Nam War.

•••

A chill runs through us when Tom tells us in 1967 that he himself is being sent to Vietnam as an information officer. Before he leaves in May, we all assemble at a photographer's studio to have a family portrait taken. The convent even releases Mary Kay for the occasion. Our smiles are guarded, wreathed in gravitas, as though we know this will be the final picture of us all; the last time in a room together, speaking to each other, civilly.

A Nameless Night

Let's choose a nameless night, sometime in late 1967. The movie *Camelot* has opened. I see a matinee at The Boulevard Twins. When, in their passion, Guinevere and Lancelot betray King Arthur, I'm salty-eyed. When King Arthur finds these two beloveds have impaled him on a dilemma, my tears spill. But when his disloyal Knights ride horses over the Round Table—the Round Table, symbol of equality, harmony, peace—fracturing, then splintering, its splendor, I sob outright—noisy, uncontrollable, inconsolable. Theatre patrons turned to shush me in the dark. I, too, am shocked at my intense response.

It takes almost fifty years to recognize that what was cracking under those hooves was our dining room table.

•••

The surface of landscapes comes from below. The sixties shifted our tectonics. Crack to chasm to canyon broke open, unspannable.

Our dining room went nightmare, its rosy walls grayed, then blackened with flung blood. The weight and rage and passion of the fight shook us to the core: warring over war. No sidelines. Anywhere you stood, earth tore.

•••

That nameless night, I come home for a hoped-for ordinary dinner, knowing dinners are no longer ordinary. That nameless night, one of many identical preceding nights, one of many repetitively following nights, but with its own specific wounds.

•••

Mom and Dad are drinking martinis with dinner; John sips bourbon. Since earning his gold watch for not smoking or drinking until his eighteenth birthday last February, he is making up for lost time.

Mom and Dad make no bones about this. I drink a Tab; milk for Jim and Ro. I can't wait to tell everyone about seeing Camelot, but before I can, Mom says:

"We're looking forward to seeing Mary at Thanksgiving, John."

"Oh well, she's really busy, Mom. Papers due, her job and everything."

"Did you invite her?"

"No—I—that is—"

"We haven't seen her in a while. Is everything—?"

"She's tired of taking the bus, okay? I told her I can't support GM and big oil and what they do to people, and if someone as smart as she is doesn't understand. then it's not my fault. Anyway, I have to practice. I may have a gig at the Scholar." John says.

I'm impressed. "On the West Bank? That's great, John. I heard Leo Kottke there. When? Are you singing, too? Need backup?"

"Just guitar. Pretty soon. I'll let you know. A guy's teaching me fiddle, too."

Mom dabs her lips with her paper napkin. (Only Dad merits a cloth one.)

"How are your classes coming, Son?" Dad wants to know. Uh-oh.

"Frankly, not worth going to. The profs are all windbags. Textbooks dull as the students. Nothing's relevant."

Dad puts down his knife. "What are we paying for, then? If you don't go to class, your student deferment won't hold."

"I've told you, Dad, I'm not deferring service. I'm *never* going."

"If you're drafted, you'll go. In this house we respect the law."

"Not if it's an unjust law."

"If you don't like it, get a degree, get elected and *change* the law. Until then you must obey it."

"I must obey my conscience. At least that's what you taught me."

Jim and Ro and I exchange looks. Better bolt our food and beat a retreat.

We were accustomed to friction—it gave a discussion its traction. Dad played devil's advocate to sharpen up our minds. But at some point, things took an ugly turn, as if he had sons to burn.

"I understand if you're afraid, Son—"

"I'm not afraid. I don't want to go to war."

"No one wants to go to war. We were as anti-war as you kids. But Hitler had to be stopped."

"There's no Hitler in Viet Nam. It's civil war in a tiny country that's no threat to us, of no strategic importance—"

All my life, Father had Known Best. But John had a point.

"He's right, Dad. It was different for you. I read Anne Frank, but—"

"Civil war my eye. They fall to the Communists, other countries will topple."

Dad's *ignoring* me.

"'The Domino Theory is bull," John growls.

"Watch your language. It happened with the Nazis."

"Maybe Communism's fairer anyway. Equal distribution of wealth instead of clutched in a few dirty hands."

"You want another Berlin Wall? Missiles in Cuba, fifty miles from us? This isn't a chess game, Son. Where's your common sense? You won the 'Voice of Democracy Contest' last year, for Pete's sake."

Mom beams. "We're still proud, Dear. Why, when our representative read your speech into the *Congressional Record*—"

"That's what opened my eyes, Dad. When I went to the regionals in Chicago, I took myself to the South Side. Horrifying. And after the finals in DC, I saw the slums. In our nation's *capital*. You can't believe how people live—the filth, the windows blasted out. Democracy's just words."

"That's my point! You have to back it up with your courage and your service if you're called up."

"I'll do community service, but I won't carry a gun."

"See, Dad? He's like our Prussian ancestor, right? Who threw down his rifle and wouldn't fight any more? It's in our blood."

I'm siding with John? But I've never seen Dad so fierce, so
unyielding—bullying John. As John bullied me. As the US bullies that
little country. Did I wish it on him? Would Dad bully me if I found the
balls to disagree?

But John, that man of peace, is a wicked fighter.

"Tom might die over there! Don't you even care?"

A short pause as his blade finds its mark. "I am proud of his choice.
Your brother is a brave man. Know why he became a paratrooper? He
was afraid of heights. Jumped out of planes 'til he got over it. And then
he enlisted."

"I can't help it if he's a fool."

How could John say that? I yank his arm. "John! Shut up!"

"He's in Viet Nam defending your freedom to be a
heartless ignoramus."

This is bad. "Dad, please—"

They butt heads like creatures prehistoric, shaking the very ground.
Mom's face is a braid of heartache. We glut our bellies, gnaw our nails,
fall mute as their voices rise.

"Tom's not afraid to fight."

"*I'm* not afraid to fight; I just want to fight for what I believe in. This
war isn't even declared."

"We're not privy to classified information, as it should be. You don't
know beans."

"I know it cost 4.5 billion dollars this year, money that should go to
health and housing and education, not slaughtering peasants scrambling
in the hills, defending their lives. Not, by the way, holing up like you
guys in some Navy destroyer."

I cannot breathe for shock. Our hallowed dinner table has
degenerated into desolate foreign terrain two strangers battle over.
Each deluded, convinced he can convince the other, if only he hurts
him enough.

Dad is silent, one hand a fist, temple veins visibly pulsing. Don't
have a heart attack, please. Don't slug John.

"You. Don't. Know. A Damn Thing. We were not holed up. I was on deck every day supervising the guns, the men. North Atlantic. South Pacific. Omaha Beach. Japan. You think I don't know what war is? What it does? We watched the Susan B. Anthony sink. You watch a ship die, it's sacred.

"Two weeks after the A-bomb I was in Hiroshima. Just ash and wilted steel. People picking through rubble like blackbirds in a wheat field. The blast drove a stem of straw into concrete. I'll never forget. Just sticking out.

"But love of my God and my country and my family is stronger even than that, Son. Even than war."

"Veterans don't even believe in this war. They marched on Washington—a hundred thousand—"

I want to slug him myself. "John. Let it alone. Can we sing a little?"

John ignores me, goes into the kitchen to refill his glass.

Stunned into silence from the start, Jim and Ro grab their escape. "What say we do the dishes, Ro? May we be excused?"

A nod suffices. They clear the table and head into the kitchen. I know they want to calm John down, and I know it's useless. I want to leave, too, but my own delusion is that I think I can help somehow. Explain them to each other. Remind them, maybe, who they are. Or were.

John comes back waving a box of plastic wrap.

"Dow Chemical! How can we even have this Saran Wrap in the house?"

He throws it on the floor.

"Pick that up. Show your mother some respect."

John retrieves it. "These are the people who make napalm, Dad. Which they blast on mothers and children like scalding honey. The screams, the smell of burning flesh—"

Mom pales, stands shakily. "I'm going to get a little bicarb of soda, and go on up. Good night."

She leaves.

"I hate this! I hate this!" I shout. "If anybody really loved peace, they'd shut up!"

I run upstairs, bang my door shut.

Underneath my feet their voices boom: Dad's thunderous professional artillery alternates with John's higher submachine-gun staccato.

Though only some words rise, all of the emotion does.

"Values...crapper!"

"...human life."

I try to read. Shut up shut up we plug our ears, we swallow our fears and shut up.

"...Your mother...you're no help...Sleep 'til noon...job...discipline!"

"...Bellyful!...military academy...demerits...federal inspection..."

Oh God, should I go down? Can I do anything? I crack open my bedroom door as John bellows:

"Only difference is you don't have to memorize Thomas Aquinas and Advanced Calculus and two centuries of English literature in the jungle. Just shoot people and come home in a body bag."

"Thin ice, Buster. Skating on thin ice."

"Sorry if facts upset you. Suffering upsets me. Did your heart stop feeling when you had your heart attack?" Oh, John.

"That's enough! Get out of my house. Stay somewhere else tonight. Maybe in Canada with the flock of chickens." Oh, Dad.

"I won't run away. I'll get Conscientious Objector status and stay here and fight."

"Not here. Not tonight."

"Fine."

The front door slams like a crack of thunder. Like a cracking table.

•••

I rummage in the rubble of those years piecing out portraits from the chips and crush. What could sap away Dad's love for his son? A son's love for his father?

Dad must have seen his ghost in John: feelings it took a lifetime to stifle or to train or drain; terrors Dad had calmed in himself by leading his men in the war. But he couldn't give John orders or reason with him or lead him anywhere.

John must have seen his ghost in Dad: he fought like someone who would never give up fighting, who never saw the irony of waging war for peace. Like a guerilla with grenades and sniper shots, he ambushed Dad, goaded him, threw human history in his face. Dad crushed him like a cigarette.

From the firestorm of blame, table linen burst in flame. Who was right was all that mattered. Childhood, like a china vessel, shattered.

Dad's Plaid

At some point there is nothing more to say. John wins his CO status and he moves away.

Then Dad scalds sweet peaceful Jim.

"Should I go back into officer's training at the military academy?" he asks.

Dad says yes.

"Okay then, Dad. Thanks."

"You always agree with me! You never fight me like your brothers do. You're not a man. You're a coward."

Crushed his heart like steel wool dropped underfoot, something to strip floors with. Could you not see the hollow witness of his eyes? How many wars did you want in the house?

This man was not the father I grew up with.

•••

Sweep the landscape clean with rushes of trauma: as they bury, earthquakes equally reveal. The stones are but a pile of rubble I arrange to suit myself.

What is Dad and what is me, what is America, what is the movies?

•••

My brothers tell me that Dad pushed them to succeed, that money was the crucial measure. I'm told he was cold. The way my brothers grew, it must be true. I see cruelty in him in later years—scarring Jim, prodding sore spots in John, or even on occasion, Mom.

But I never was the object of his push and chill. My body was a walking invitation for cruelty, yet never once did I suffer at his hands.

It was if he felt his girls were extra credit, but he'd be tested on the boys.

•••

In its many stripes and colors, authority ran like a plaid grid through Dad's life—and he loved it as only someone answerable to it can. From the supremacy of God and eternal verity of Catholicism to the majesty of our legal system; from the military's crystal hierarchy to the natural hegemony of fatherhood, authority inspired, defined, and ultimately defeated him. He obeyed it, identified with it, earned it, was certain of it. But as his children grew and his celebrity dried up, in large measure he lost authority, and in so doing, lost a large part of himself. Authority itself lost authority in the sixties—our President gunned down, our Church transformed, rioting in the streets, police and military taunted by protestors. No one was more shocked than my father.

When the Minnesota Department of Economic Development offered Dad a job as a celebrity ambassador for Minnesota tourism, he jumped at it like a smallmouth bass.

He'd loved our yearly trips up north and he loved to sell what he believed in. Now he'd sell Minnesota.

He's issued a car, State seal gleaming on its door, so that he can drive around to small towns and resort areas, greeting his public and offering the Department's advice for attracting tourists.

Released from the claustrophobic booth, and stimulated by the beauty of the landscapes and the warmth of the people, he thrives.

I see him now in his marked state car—holding his pipe by the bowl, speaking into it as if it were a microphone, causing passing speeders to slow down, G-Man to the end.

Within a few years, he's so successful that he's appointed head of the whole state agency. A nice bump to his authority, but it sadly means, of course, less time on the road and more time pushing paper.

The late sixties cascade change.

Pogo marries a woman of keen intelligence but whose feelings toward the family fluctuate. They live in the Twin Cities.

Tom, still in Viet Nam, misses their wedding, but is back in 1968 to marry his own sweetheart, his best friend's kid sister, Linda. Like many veterans, he can't yet talk about his military experiences overseas. He's had enough of Army life and just wants out, like our Prussian ancestor. He wants to start his own business, be his own boss. He applies for a discharge. But Tom's a good officer. They won't let him go. Instead, they promote him and say, "Resubmit in a couple of years." He and Linda are transferred to a base in Virginia.

Pogo's first son is born; Tom's arrives the following year. I head off to college.

Kako leaves the convent. John is a writhing mass of disrespect. What's the world coming to?

Dad loves a good argument, but has no sparring partners left. Jim won't engage. Tourism isn't enough. Grandchildren aren't enough. Where's heroism? Where are the pleasures of life? No pipe—Dad's doc took him off tobacco, put him on a stricter diet. Just two kids left to take on vacation. He visits his father in Nebraska. Like Gobby, Grandpa went "senile." "I never want to go that way," Dad says grimly.

His face resembles Gable in *The Misfits*, scarred with pain and loss, but still the boss.

Gibraltar Topples

After a dark freshman year at a Catholic girl's college in Madison, Wisconsin, I transfer to the University of Minnesota.

I am reading in my bedroom one warm summer night in 1972 when Mom shouts from their bedroom.

"Help! Help!"

I plunge into their room—Dad can't get his breath. I phone the rescue squad, which arrives quickly and spirits the two of them off to the hospital. Jim and Ro and I follow in the car.

When we reach the hospital, they've put him in intensive care.

"Your father is alive, but he has congestive heart failure," says the doctor.

"Doesn't failure mean it stopped? But he's alive."

The doctor clarifies: "His heart is working, but not well."

Dad looks terrible: gray-faced, tube up his nose. I want to protect his dignity.

He's hospitalized for five days. We're badly shaken. Mortality is not a word we associate with Dad.

When he's home and recovering, we have gentle conversations.

This unnerved him, too. He makes a point of saying he's had a happy life. He talks of mom with tears in his eyes: how he loved her, how she hurt, how we must be kind to her.

"Sure, Dad. But you're doing fine."

Early that November, my senior year, five weeks shy of turning twenty-one, I win a nice character role in a University production. Final dress rehearsal is tonight.

I live in a crummy but autonomous little studio apartment near the campus, but today I decide to leave my morning class early and take the bus home to Tangletown.

It's not even clear to me why I'm making this hour-long trip. Certainly not to press my opening night outfit—I'd have to carry it back on the bus. I'd come home a few days earlier to repack my stage makeup in Dad's old unused tackle box. There's no reason to come home, so why? Maybe I just wanted to stroke the old dining room table and get some good luck vibes from the folks.

Rounding the curve, I know instantly why I've come. Red lights flash across the face of our white house. I tear across the lawn and up the steps.

The dining room is full of men in uniform, in white and blue. Pogo's here, too. Mom is weeping in his arms.

"What happened? What happened?" I am asking. It's the ambulance, it's the rescue squad. "Is everything okay?"

And no one answers. No one answers. Like I'm not there.

An anonymous uniform says, "It's your father. Your father. We did all we could do."

My father. *My father.*

I split in two.

•••

They did all that they could do. I must do all that I can do. I must go hug my mother. I sidle past my brother.

I try to comfort her and fail. I am not tall enough, nor am I male. She doesn't see or know me.

So this is death.

I take a breath.

Half an orphan now. Gather up the others. Ro and Jim and John.

I drive to the high school, gather up my broken melting baby sister. On to campus to pull Jim out of freshman English. He looks up from his desk; our eyes meet through the glass in the classroom door. He knows at once, and starts to cry. As do we. Liquid with grief.

We drive to the hippie-house on the West Bank. A fellow war-resister answers the flaking door and shouts for John, who descends halfway down the spooling staircase.

We tell him. He says nothing. Does not move. His glaze of silence will last for years, barren of tears.

•••

At home, in between sorrow-choked phone calls and plans, I remember my dress rehearsal. No understudies. But must the show really go on?

My siblings encourage me: "You should do it. If you want." "Dad would want you to." "We'll be fine."

Performing. Something I know how to do. Unlike everything else now.

So I do. It's the ultimate dinner table play, whose warm and philosophical central character, Grandpa, is like Dad at his best: *You Can't Take It With You.*

After rehearsal, I grab a few things from my apartment and get a ride home from a friend.

Mom's in bed, Pogo's gone, Tom and Mary Kay are flying in. John— stony, tearless—turns in early. We three Youngers stay up late that night, sprawling in the living room, holding our personal Irish wake, remembering details, telling old stories. Suddenly we're electrified by a sound not heard for ten years: The broken grandmother clock.

Bong.

Bong.

Bong.

We gape at it, agog. No one is anywhere near it. It broke years ago and was never repaired. The time on its beautiful face has been stuck at 2:50.

Bong.

Bong.

Bong.

The hands drop to 6:30. Unbelievable. Spines shivering like xylophones, we stare at one another.

Twelve

Thirteen,

Fourteen.

More. Way too many.

Scary, yet delicious. An unmistakable message from Dad.

Years later, when Mom dies, the clock in Ro's house will stop at 2:50.

•••

The funeral home, the rosary, all a blur. Relatives and cards come flooding in to her, who lost her marriage and her best friend in a day; weeping, weaving in each other's arms a nest of grief, all but stiff and stone-eyed John, numbed by the war in our home.

The Mass I can't recall, but I wore white, affirmation of all that is ongoing, having seen Dad glowing in a dream. Even science holds that energy can neither be created nor destroyed. Even science, I think to myself. In my heart I know the him of him is not so dead.

But my body knows death, from my dad's forehead. It is cold, it is final, it is all they say it is. A shock you never get over: when you feel with your lips that warmth has flown.

My mother quivering in black like Jackie—all I recall are the moving reflections of leafless branches over the limousine hood rushing at me, entering my chest.

•••

He's honored with a veteran's burial at Fort Snelling, firm triangle of flag placed in Mom's trembling arms, something to hold. It rains every day for a month.

I move home for a while.

After the funeral, the dozen carrot cakes, the homeward flights, John's wordless departure (will he never break down and cry?) after the thank-you notes, the play's last performance, the dwindling phone calls, the on-getting of life in the quieting house, it starts to sink in: a heart attack. At fifty-nine. Dead in his own bed, reading an unlikely bestseller: Jonathan Livingston Seagull. Certainly loosened your soul, that book.

Incapacitated by grief, Mom stays in bed. We three youngest of the Youngers, weakened, weeping, drawn to one another, plunging our faces in his clothes to catch his fading smell, what was his voice like where was his laugh? Remember the way he said chocolate? What was the last thing he said to you?

A day or two before he died, after packing up my makeup in the old tacklebox, I stop into their room for a bit of advice. Mom's asleep.

•••

"Dad, I'm thinking about cutting my hair," I whisper. "Should I?"
"No matter how you wear it, you'll always be beautiful."
I smile. "Aw, Dad. Thanks. Good night."
Our last conversation.

•••

Outlived by your own father, Dad, you spared yourself your larger fears: senility, incompetence, incontinence; you died with the lion within you alive.

Each pain withdraws, compacts, compresses. Each joy expands. The subtle force of memory forms these family lands; upheavals, the continuous melody of life, the urge to leave this country and to revisit it form these lands.

Flash floods rush through the landscape sweep away the crumbling houses.

I see your green gray eyes parting the leaves for a look, your voice a part of nature.

The flower thanks the gardener.

Yet here's a picture of a you I never knew, under the wing of a Piper Cub, wolf pelt by your side.

Why did your heart break? Why could you not love my brothers as you loved me?

What is you and what is me? What is the myth our lives are telling?

What are the symbols of our time? What is America, what is the movies?

Montana, Day Six: Focus

The next morning, dawn cracks and we're up at it.

Mike changes our seating arrangements. The boys patch our leaky raft and also realize that it is lighter than the hefty one they've been propelling, and consequently less reliable. Also, Jim's crew sported two people over sixty and one advancing on it. The younger, more powerful paddlers were all in the other raft.

"You and Ro get in the hefty one with Don and Derek. We'll take this one. Domenic wants to try the pontoon."

I'm scared for us, scared for him, scared for everyone.

But scared doesn't help. Focus helps. This will be over in a day or two. Meanwhile, dammit, Irene, look around.

Glorious, unperturbed mountains. Brushy vigorous firs. Sheets of luminous river.

And these remarkable people. All working so hard, being so affable. And no one is asking me to patch and pump the rafts. Elderhood has its advantages.

Wilderness and humans illuminate each another.

Sibland

A family is a landscape of its own, as granted as the earth and trees: a wild ecology of feelings, unique in balance, particular of circulation. Each person, each event becomes environment, familiar, dear and scary.

Each element's essential in a landscape: none moved, removed without a subtle or a drastic change. No force shies from the landscape— all times and changes carried off by elemental forces which transform the hardest substances to soft.

Patterns marked in rock, in soil, in surface give a landscape its identity.

Emotion is the weather of the family, patterning the faces, the voices, and the hearts.

•••

A family is a landscape changing scope and light and season. One day the father is a mountain peak sheltering a gentle mother river and the next the father is a fallen pine by a dried riverbed and scattered children rocks.

Dad worked in landslides; Mom in abrasion, erosion. Either way, trees fall.

•••

A landscape is a thing you find yourself in. It's hardly a thing you're aware you have entered until it gets dramatic.

Measures Taken

Unlike the tear-swamped rest of us, John did not break down and cry after Dad died. He stopped speaking altogether. His body went rigid. He blinked very little.

"It's like he's catatonic," we thought. We kept thinking it was only a matter of time before he released his grief.

There were so many details to attend to—Mom to care for, and our own shock and grief, to say nothing of distributing those dozen carrot cakes brought by thoughtful neighbors.

I moved back in to be with the family, but John stayed at his commune.

"When I went to visit," Tom remembers, "I took John by the hand to pull him out of his chair. When I let go, his arm just stood out in midair. I couldn't believe this, so I lifted John's arm above his head. It stayed. Just stayed sticking straight up in the air."

In those wound-fresh days, John came home to Tangletown from time to time, sometimes to hang out with us silently, sometimes to play a song or two.

I was not at home in January when John finally broke down, so I don't know how it happened, what he said, or what brought him to the moment he agreed to get outpatient mental help at Minneapolis' General Hospital.

The day before he started treatment, Mom left for California to visit Tom, Linda, and their young sons: three-year-old Don and infant David. (The Army had rejected Tom's resubmit, promoted him again, and sent them to the most beautiful Army base in the country, in Monterey.)

Another mother might have waited. But another mother wasn't ours.

By March, I move back to my apartment and get a job in food service at the U of M Hospital. Starting at 5 a.m., I load up a stainless steel hot cart and serve meals to psychiatric patients. After cleanup, I get back to my basement apartment around 12:30, in time for later classes and rehearsal. When I am cast on the Centennial Showboat, the University's floating summer theatre, I begin socking away enough money so that I can quit the hospital when rehearsals begin.

One hot afternoon, just before I need to leave for rehearsal, I'm startled by a banging on my front door.

I open it. John barges in.

"Hi, John—um—I was just on my way—"

He's always unpredictable, but today he is excited and somewhat scary. His eyes are flicky and buggy.

"I can brainwave my thoughts to you!" he cries, without even saying hello. He vigorously shoves his forehead into mine, pressing my skull to his with his strong guitarist's hands.

"Well, that's great, John," I blink and try to draw back. "I believe thoughts can move without speech—"

"Quiet! Quiet! Receive these thoughts!"

For a moment I try to receive his thoughts, but I'm afraid. His invasion of my space and the force he shows obscure whatever he's trying to accomplish.

"John, look, back off a second."

"Stop talking! We don't need to talk! We can communicate without words!"

I pull back. "I believe you, but how can you hear my thoughts if you won't even hear my voice?"

"Quiet!" Again he fiercely presses his head to mine.

"Sorry, John—I have rehearsal! You have to go now!" He does not respond, just continues straining his head against mine. I don't like this, I want to have a spiritual belief about it, but I am afraid, afraid, and now I'm going to be late.

"Stop it! John, if you're reading my thoughts you know I have to leave."

I pull away again.

"Why do foreheads even have to press together to read thoughts anyway? Can't it be done from a distance?"

He says nothing, nor does he budge.

I hate this. I have to get him out and I don't want him here when I get back.

"Just stop! You have to go! I have to leave!"

Still no response, just intense flicky eyes. Now I am screaming.

"Get out! Get Out! GET OUT!"

I scream at him again and again. After an eternity, he moves to and then out the door, dulled, like a large beast slowly leaving a watering hole.

I'm shaking. A rotten stew of horrible feelings—yelling at him, being afraid of him, afraid *for* him, guilty for feeling threatened by my own brother, shock that it took him so long to get the message.

What's wrong with him? What's wrong with him?

The theatre is a great place to channel emotional confusion, and get congratulated for it. I go to rehearsal.

A few months later, Mom gets a call. The police have delivered John to the state asylum in Fergus Falls, a small town 180 miles northwest of Minneapolis, after finding him on a park bench there shouting, "I renounce Satan! I renounce Satan!"

Somehow I am able to get away to visit him in this icky sad green-walled institution. He looks awful. Green walls look bad on everybody.

"It was bad dope. Must have been laced with angel dust."

I want to believe him, but I have had my own recent scare with him. Still, I've read *One Flew Over the Cuckoo's Nest*; I'm torn between wanting to spring him and seeing if there's a medical way to help. Do people get better in these places?

Soon afterwards, Pogo convinces Mom we have to commit John to a mental institution, not just this temporary business in Fergus Falls. He initiates legal proceedings.

The hearing takes place that October. Having to testify is excruciating. What a betrayal. It's not like John's looney-looney. He's brilliant. He may be spiritually advanced in some way—ahead of his time.

But I never want a replay of his enforced telepathy.

"Is your brother's behavior normal?" the lawyer asks me.

"Well, not all of it might be considered normal."

If only John weren't here in the courtroom. He'll know I betrayed him.

"Do you think he'd benefit from treatment? Remember you are under oath."

"I guess I think I hope treatment might be helpful for him. He isn't all that happy. He did scare me. But I don't think it's permanent. I don't think he's a real danger to people or to himself. If you do decide to commit him, I hope you will reevaluate him after a few months, because he's really smart and that may be all that's going on."

I'm sick to my stomach with conflict.

John is admitted to Anoka Asylum, which in those days fit the classic profile of gothic, terrifying nuthouse. (Even today, now defunct as a medical facility, it's used as a Halloween haunted house.) Thorazine and other drugs are administered against his will. Only Mom and Ro visit him. Neither drives so they must take several busses to do so. I am working, going to classes, and performing. I do not visit.

He is released after a few months, for "good behavior." He tells Ro he played the game of the good patient.

John never spoke to me of this experience at length, except to spit fury.

"How could you do this to me?"

"We were worried about you."

"You have no idea what it's like to be restrained against your will! And no one came to visit but Mom and Ro!"

"We didn't have a car! And I was working, taking classes, and performing every night!"

I am not fully conscious of how I fear him.

Mercury

When it comes time to bid farewell to Tangletown, Mom chooses a little condo near downtown; the three Olders chip in to buy it for her.

The day of the estate sale, we drop Mom at her new place: blue velvet chairs, delicate new furniture. "It doesn't have to be childproof!" she crows. At day's end, a few of us return, find the liquidators have trashed Mom's wedding sash on the lawn with other unsalables. We enter our ghostly house. Farewell, flying steps. Feel the thrusting absence of the dining room table, pity the sunroom, bereft of its desk and magnificent typewriter.

And then we scatter from the fracture of Dad's death like mercury from a snapped thermometer. Away from the mother lode/load.

•••

Now out of the convent, Mary Kay has learned to write checks, pay rent, wear makeup, and hold down a job. Sick of Minnesota winters, she buys herself a white Mustang and moves to southern California to work for the Department of Defense (!). Her obesity is still a painful issue, but she joins AA and remains sober. She will never marry.

Stationed now in northern California and five years from retiring with a full pension, Tom can no longer stand the Army. They finally accept his resignation. Always money-smart, he buys real estate. He and Linda rear their two boys with practical wisdom, teaching them to raise chickens and use computers.

"Whatever the future brings, they'll benefit from one skill or the other," Tom reasons. (Both Don and David grow up to be tech whizzes and make good livings from their computer knowledge.) Don, his eldest, eventually takes a rafting trip to Montana with his own son Derek and daughter Lauren.

Once John is released from the asylum, he hightails it West, where he works off his alternative draft service fighting forest fires. On completing his duty, he moves to Washington state, builds himself a cabin in the wild, and spends a year alone like Thoreau, albeit much further from civilization. He then moves to Portland where he becomes a leading classical guitarist and teacher.

Jim heads west as well and marries a sharp wise Montana woman. His father-in-law Bill, a doctor, warns him that her juvenile diabetes predicts a short life.

"I'll take whatever time I can get with her," says Jim. Though plagued with various medical challenges, they enjoy many years together rearing their three boys as Jim practices law. He and the boys learn backcountry skills and survival on frequent trips with tough taskmaster Bill, and make use of them on one particularly memorable rafting trip on the South Fork of the Flathead.

The West calls Ro, too. After college, she also moves to Montana, then on to Seattle, where she meets and marries a brilliant and sensitive lawyer. They move to Portland, raise two remarkable artists. She finds her creativity and serenity teaching Waldorf kindergarten.

I move to New York to pursue acting, then writing. I marry a wonderful man who both acts and writes. I gain and lose weight for decades until therapy and inner work brings me to balance.

Mom by now wakes up with a crossword puzzle and a gin-and-orange-juice, refreshing both throughout the day. She tops it off with wretched, repetitious phone calls to whomever of us answers.

Her affronts to me continue. Oh my Belfast, my Jerusalem.

After my sixty-pound loss, she sends me a huge muumuu for Christmas. It's covered with multi-colored fruits with bites taken out of them. "If you lose too much weight, aren't you afraid of losing your rings?" she asks.

She breaks her own cardinal rule—"Never wear white to a wedding; it's the bride's day"—by packing a cream lace dress to wear to my wedding when she knows I will be wearing a cream lace dress.

As far from Mom as we could get—Mary Kay, Tom, John, Jim, Ro, and I all find peace in forming new family landscapes of traumas and glories, forests of stories not mine to tell.

And what of our eldest brother?

The Determined Empty Chair

The brilliant firstborn Irish son who took up the mantle of fame from my father and swung it over bigger markets, Pogo remains a determined empty chair at the table.

When I meet him in dreams, it's always a happy reunion, a reminder we're more than mortal, that chronology's not everything.

I want to leave him back in the "Pogo-Bogo, Reen-Bean" days, in his crack-skull Family Journal adolescence, his goofy "be kind to your web-footed friends, for a duck may be somebody's brother" jokiness, or even in the heyday of his fame, hobnobbing with cultural bigshots, scoring an honorary degree from a most prestigious university. He got further on the upward outward ladder of public success than any of us.

But I can't leave him there. He left us first.

Was it true Dad pushed him to succeed, and money was the only measure? Did he swallow that hook, line, and sinker, a hardened vein of money hunger constricting his poet's compassionate heart?

Mom told us he suggested at Dad's death that she would save a lot of money by burying him in a pine box.

A horrifying slap to her grief. "He was an important man in Minneapolis," she counters. "I won't compromise his dignity."

It isn't only money, though.

Shockingly, not long after Dad's death, his wife writes Mom a scathing letter, ostensibly as part of her own psychotherapy. She insists Mom is relying too heavily on Pogo since Dad died.

"He's *my* husband, not yours," she writes.

We all have our issues with Mom, but there's such a thing as human decency.

Is it Pogo's wife who urges and wedges him away from us? Shortly thereafter, he comes to Mom's apartment and tears all his pictures out of the family scrapbook, destroying the gift Kako made for Mom and Dad's twenty-fifth anniversary, further rending Mom's raw heart.

He takes a job in a larger Midwestern city, where they move with their two young sons.

Over the years they run hot and cold with us, returning to the fold occasionally, when they want something (the grandmother clock, or career help for a son), then abruptly cutting off contact.

We talk among ourselves, trying to understand what happened this time, or why he chafingly persists in calling siblings by their baby names, why he exploded his close bond with Tom, how he could believe the help I gave his son was intended to smash their relationship.

•••

Acts of love, Pogo, were ground under your heel. You were a punch to the solar plexus, an onslaught of nausea. I understand "cold shoulder," for you turned from my open arms at a family funeral, launching a rocket of ice.

But must I list disappointments? Bad behavior? Misplaced values? Delusions?

Must I use you to shock and entertain, to get people on my side?

•••

One morning I get a phone call from Tom's wife Linda.

"We thought you should know that Pogo has been lost in the woods for two days."

"What?"

"Went on a hike and didn't return. They're sending out helicopters."

I leave a message on their answering machine: "Just heard—hope everything's okay—thinking of you and sending love."

Big search. They find him on the third day, walking, weak and dehydrated. He'd wandered off the trail, lost his way. Had to filter puddle water through his baseball cap, make a shivery bed of moss and dead tree, confront mortality.

I leave a message when he's found, assuming near-death yields perspective. It does: he reconnects with other siblings. But not with me.

Years go on, stings subside.

The rest of us get closer, visit more often. We feel sorry Pogo and his wife miss out.

•••

Even if life has somehow charred your poet's heart, I see you happily in dreams. If you called tomorrow, I would answer. There's no reason not to love, no time for anything else.

Love may mean distance. Children pout in bedrooms. Doesn't mean we leave the house. Doesn't mean we leave the landscape. Nothing is permanent, eventually.

Maladroit

Oh, siblings.

Who knows what the roots are doing, dislodging, under the surface, disturbing the tonnage of soil, disintegrating rock itself grabbing for moisture, blood, love?

In the early seedbed no feelings were concealed. We tried out everything in honesty: we whacked and banged against each other, poked and twisted wrists, hertz-donutted, and how far does your thumb bend back and how many freckles on your arm how loud can I cup my hands and yell in your ear inch me and pinch me were walking across a bridge build volcanoes in the sandbox burying the hose making igloos back by the garage side by side, never questioning our comradeship despising it at times, of course, in the utter free play of emotion, whole flow: you feel it, you say it, you watch it go.

All the emotions of Shakespeare were not more succinct: Wait up I'm gonna tell I hate you Stop it That's mine I was here first Can I come Ow Look what I got Don't I am not Mom It's not fair What are you doing I'm sorry Oh ick Gimme that.

Once so easy of expression with each other—our words like flattened cardboard boxes slicking us down snowy hills: you feel it, you say it, you let it go.

But in the eighties, we're clumsy with each other. Snow melted, leaving gouges, rough ground. Tread with caution, catch on vegetation, twist ankles on unseen roots.

We live vast geographies apart; visits are rare, phone calls occasional (oftener with Ro, now close to me as skin), between twos for news, and that stammery, oddly syncopated, yearly Christmas conference call.

Sometimes gladness takes us deep into the night, past competing puns and old sore spots. Beloved family cadences pull up the memories; our hearts rise like popovers.

But we share a wariness, for sooner or later, by commission or omission, in real or in imagined ways, we hurt each other, then intensify the pain with silence.

Underground rivers marsh up, muddy the walkways, secret feelings welling.

How could he say that? Why is it always her? He didn't even listen.

Conversation encumbered with subtext. Are you angry and not telling me? Will what I say be used against me? For the good of the family, shall I hint that someone's angry with you? Shall I assume responsibility for smoothing that relationship, for making peace? Who's talking to Mom at the moment? What is she saying about me? Does silence do more or less damage? What is the good of the family?

With spouses or siblings (excluding the one in question, of course), we phone or gather, dissect character and motivation. Dominant and recessive angst, inner rooms heaping with psychic debris.

Angers, errors, conflicts, guilt: pass the basket round, take yours, pass it on.

Life is weathers passing over, coloring rock and lake and clover. Day or night, which is right?

And yet there's such a thing as human decency.

Montana, Day Six:
Aiming for Hazards

Don is a calmer, more specific navigator. Then again, he's Tom's son. His father was so much kinder than Jim's was to him.

"We're aiming for that rusty pine on shore."

Counterintuitive, but we trust him. We aim for it and he rudders us away from it.

"Aim for that big rock. We'll go left of it, but aim right at it."

It's hard to get used to aiming for hazards, but with power at the rudder, it works so well.

More perilous rock gardens. Out of the raft to portage again. I can't hold on to the raft as we traverse them, because its weight pulls me forward almost to toppling.

We make the confluence of the White River. As promised, the South Fork broadens, but it also accelerates.

We flash over whitewater, waving our paddles in the air at success and to signal the other raft we made it, but only for a split second, because here comes the next hazard.

We think of rapids as water, but they are actually rocks, our hidden saboteurs. Exhilarating to get over them, but they dislodge and spin and confuse and toss us out of the rafts, and there is no steering clear of this clamoring river population.

Lauren wants to try the pontoon. She does fine for a while but then gets swept into shallows. We pick her up at an exposed rocky island where we stop for lunch.

We munch chocolate and nuts and pee behind a hunk of rocks. It feels good to rest the muscles, to look at the sunny mountains.

"Horsetails followed by fishscales," says Ro, observing the clouds. "That predicts moisture."

Oh, not really. Really? We have a ways to go. It's only one-thirty. Please let us make camp before the "moisture" hits.

I try to blot out the thought of tomorrow's red danger rapids swelling with rainwater.

Ravine

Dad would have turned seventy-five that day Mom drank so much she fell. The fall shook her brain against her skull and bruised it. She lay unconscious on the condo floor for two days. The Red Cross, where she'd volunteered and now was paid to answer phones, sent someone up. They called the ambulance and us.

Four of us flew in, prepared for death, given Mom's small chance of surviving the delicate surgery. We arrived to find her hooked to life support, unconscious, but alive. We went to her apartment to spend the night.

As I walked through that door, my legs nearly gave out, Mom, looking into your life this way, the piles of dirty clothes, the unwashed tub, the dust, the dishes, and the yellow cigarette-smoke film gumming the velvet upholstery, tabletops, walls, like a sepia photograph. I thought you never cleaned our house because there were so many of us. You just didn't care about yourself enough to clean. Mopping up the pool of shit you'd lain in for two days, I thought of the sweet scalloped soaps, snow-white damask, translucent bone china of the Hotel Fontenelle.

My heart roared with pity.

You recovered, lived alone again. Stopped drinking, thanks to your medicine.

We insisted on a cleaning woman, you allowed her. Back to your TV, your smokes, and your puzzles, dancing with dukes in romantic novels. "Go out and play!" I wanted to say, but it was some ideal life for you.

This ravine between your near-death and your death gave me time to think.

I remembered years back a Sunday after Mass, pulling sweet rolls apart. The phone rings, you answer, you sink on the flying steps, crying and crying. Your brother Johnny died.

I was young enough to be confused—why were you so sad? You'd only mentioned him once or twice, he never came to visit, you never went. You hardly knew each other.

I now know that was why you mourned. No parents, no siblings. Can I forgive you for the damage you have suffered?

•••

The movement of glaciers plucks away stones. Some that are lodged in my heart you remove, leaving soft lakes in your wake that echo your voice:

> *There's nothing so beautiful in Woman as a low and gentle voice.*
> *If you have but two loaves, sell one, and buy hyacinths for the soul.*
> *I will bet a silk pajama there isn't any three-l lama.*
> *Life is real, life is earnest, and the grave is not its goal.*
> *O wad some Power the giftie gie us / To see oursels as ithers see us!*

Poetry was natural to you, part of conversation. Something Donna Reed had overlooked.

You left us manners like a lovely coat, a gift even strangers admire.

And for that school night in the middle of my tortured adolescence when you said: "You'll like this movie. Stay up and watch it with me." *An Affair to Remember.* To watch it, just the two of us, was like some tremendous dessert, salted with sniffles for star-crossed love. I was as grateful as if you had made it yourself. The love the love the love the love. The almost unbearable love.

•••

I want it to be one way or another: a wonderful dad and a horrible mother, a heart-seeking mom and a cruel dad. This won't explain the time we had.

I want it to be one way or the other. How could you approve of his ambition?

How could he approve of your neglect? How close I am to you and how you distance me.

Life is weathers passing over, coloring rock and lake and clover. Day or night, which is right? Man or woman, which is human?

•••

I find a picture of a you I never knew: sitting on one leg on a hand-hewn porch in Jackson Hole in flannel shirt and jeans, as if you belong in cowboy life. A look I've never seen before or since radiates from your young face: pure and serious confidence. You show a natural faith in the natural world and a natural self. A woman I could have befriended. I might have traveled to Montana with her.

Curious Old Path

At age seventy-five, Mom is getting erratic and confused in her phone calls. We know she isn't drinking, so one weekend we three sisters fly out to Minneapolis to assess the situation.

Her hygiene, nourishment, and housekeeping are sorely wanting. Gently, gingerly: "What do you think about assisted living, Mom?"

"Oh, I think it's time," she says. Immense relief.

•••

Lengthy sibling conference call. Who'll keep an eye on her?

Her chickens won't come home to roost.

It seems clear Pogo wants no part of the conversation or the decision.

Mary Kay flatly refuses. "I won't be the classic unmarried daughter caring for her mother."

"We don't mind Mom for a month over Christmas," say Tom and Linda, "but we don't want permanent responsibility." They keep a weather eye out for Mom's sister, Aunt Ellen, as well.

John is silent. He is scarcely caring for himself.

"Having Mom in New York isn't workable," I confess. I'm in therapy, unable to imagine a rancor-free relationship.

"We're responsible for Maggie's mom just now," Jim tells us. "Her lupus is worsening." They're also rearing three boys.

But Ro steps up to the plate. Though she and her husband Mark have two young children, "I want her near. I want to do this," she avers. We flood her with gratitude.

Ro finds a pleasant assisted-living residence close to their Portland home. The well-maintained apartments have maid service, community meals, and medical staff on site.

Available siblings sort, toss, pack, and load in Minneapolis; drive, unload, and unpack Mom's things in the new place. She's excited.

But soon Ro reports, "She's shouting at other residents, accusing them of stealing her clothes. Today she hit one of her attendants. They can't keep her there anymore."

Ro could not confide till recently that Mom was also spreading feces on the wall.

Delicate, linen-sheathed, Coty-powdered Mom. Heart-crushing.

Doctor visits and tests provide her unsurprising but official diagnosis. Betty travels the curious old path taken by not only by her grandmother, but her Aunt Irene as well: senility, now christened Alzheimer's.

Ro finds a newly-opened facility designed expressly for such patients. Subdued décor. Quiet, home-like spaces. Nurses in civvies. Coded entry to safeguard wandering patients. We move her over.

Montana, Day Six:
Curdles and Limits

Lunch over. Back on the water. Paddling. Paddling. Paddling.

Blisters on our thumb webs. Chamois cream. Wrap with black electrical tape.

After a few hours, I improvise a song to keep my muscles working, making up lyrics, consoling myself that even pirates sang heave ho to keep going.

But my muscles are tiring. The sky is darkening. Oh please no.

Portage again. Two, three times. Dodge rocks. Tedious.

Where is the campsite? Whoops, Mike missed it. We went right by it. There is no going back. We have to choose another.

The sky curdles with dark clouds. Say it ain't so. Our raingear is tightly rolled inside dry bags we can't open now. Can't chance soaking our sleeping bags.

Mike scours the shorelines for alternate campsites. While not a highly trafficked area, it is Friday night. All the mapped ones are taken. Oh my God. How will Seidlitz find us?

Hour six and fifteen miles into our paddle, immensely weary. Now, as meteorologist Ro predicted, it starts to rain. Not a sweet-summer-thank-God-it's-falling on-our-sweaty-selves rain, but a solid-cold-muscle-clenching-what-are-you-doing-here rain. We are now more than drenched. We are cold.

Cold, as we've seen, is a trigger for Ro. She can endure heat in a way I can't, but cold sends her somewhere into our Minnesota childhood, days of soggy snowsuits, mittens hidden or mismatched or still wet in the morning, toe-numbing walks to school in rubber boots that effectively transfer body heat directly into the snow and conduct icicles of cold directly up the legs, souring the heart, pressing tears from the eyes.

We're shivering. Can't be that far from a campsite, can we? At least the effort of paddling offers muscular compensation, a bit of warmth from movement.

Bright-veined lightning stabs a mountain, thunder cracks. The downpour begins in earnest—more waterfall than rain.

"Pull off! Pull off! Everybody off the water now!" A river raft is not a place to be in a storm, and this one is building.

With tremendous effort we order our rubbery muscles to pull us to shore, get out, haul the boats up, but once we're on the bank, our bodies go from warm to freezing. Can't stop teeth chattering, body trembling.

We all huddle under a pine for a bit of shelter. Ro's pale and shaking. I'm helpless to help her.

Then from his miraculous pack, Don pulls two small plastic bags.

He tears open the emergency rain poncho. We help Ro into it. It's the density of a cleaner's bag, but it sheds the rain.

The other packet holds a silver emergency blanket. In it he wraps not his kids, but Ro and me, his old aunties. It is surprisingly, welcomely warm. I practically want to cry for his thoughtfulness.

It starts to *hail*. If our jaws were not so tightly clenched, they would have dropped. This is pretty pure. A thin strip of mylar between us and The Elements, which are trying themselves out in all kinds of configurations.

Warmth. Rest. Food. Dry Clothing. Basics. None of them available now.

We don't gripe. Everyone is wet. But sure wish we hadn't missed that first campsite. It's 6 p.m. Light is fading in the mountain valley.

The hail subsides, the rain lets up slightly.

"Let's take our chance now," Mike says. "It might get stronger, but we've got to make a break for it. The map shows a campsite not too far off."

Back down the hill, the ubiquitous slippery rocks, shove the rafts back on the water, take up our paddles again. The rain still broadly falls, but the lightning has business elsewhere for the moment.

And of course the rapids are still rapids, we still have to pay attention and pull and curve and try to avoid stone shores and projectiles but soon, we know, soon we'll be out.

And indeed, it is true, within an hour a splendid campsite comes into view. Perfectly situated on a promontory above the river—but wait, is that smoke? Yes.

Hell. There must be a dozen people up there. They've erected a giant tarp and have a blazing fire going. They wave and toast us with their beer cans as we pass.

Our hearts are so heavy they almost swamp the boat. We have to paddle on.

Just then, an impossible-to-see feisty rock protrudes. Our raft runs into it, Ro gets tossed out again. Her leg goes under the raft. I see by her bloodless face she is at the limits of her tolerance, of her physicality. She's cold, she's in pain, please don't break her knee.

This tips me into my limit. I shout to Mike, "This Is Enough! Enough! We have to stop!"

"Okay we'll stop, we'll find some kind of campsite. Pull up everybody!"

Mike's crew is already farther downriver, swirling around a bend, but our crew has stopped.

Ever so gingerly Don helps Ro extract her leg from under the raft. It will sport a huge bruise, but—mercifully—nothing worse.

"Why don't you two make your way back to that campsite?" Don suggests.

"Those folks will let you get warm by their fire while we set up our campsite."

"No, no," I say. "Let's go straight to our site so we don't have to walk back over these horrible rocks."

For indeed, the rocks along this shore are the most treacherous yet: grapefruit and cantaloupe-sized, slick with algae and plant life. Perfect anklebreakers.

I begin singing an old affirmation quietly to myself: *I create my reality, the present is my point of power.*

After ten minutes on this difficult path, we're within shouting distance of the other raft.

Mike calls out, "Go back to the other campsite. Get warm at their fire while we set up camp and start making dinner."

We almost burst into tears, but any kind of warmth sounds good right now.

So we turn around. Back, step by step over the precarious rock. Don holds Ro's arm. I am just slowly, slowly proceeding.

There's a massive rock promontory between this stony shore and the path leading up to the campsite. The beach ceases altogether here— it's just a pool of green water. Looking up, I spot on the promontory fairly regular ledge-y handholds and footholds.

"We could climb up it rather than go around if you want. Looks pretty doable."

"No!" Ro says. "I can't. I can't climb up there."

"Okay, okay, no problem—just trying to make it easier."

The cold rain still falls. Calf deep already, we start inching around the promontory. With each step it gets deeper and colder. This water lives at the base of this stone and never warms.

To our knees. To our thighs. To our waists. When the icy water covers my breasts, an inner alarm goes off. I am colder and more miserable now than I have been in all my life. This is the nadir of exertion and expectation. How much deeper is this pool? To my neck? Will we drown?

Between Here and Heaven

In a culture whose primary values are caffeine-driven, where what you know is who you are, where measurement and date and logic and sequence and precision are sacrosanct, the presence and progress of Alzheimer's reads as unqualified tragedy. Everyday values, skills, recognition, and protocol recede before our eyes, leaving a stranger in the eroded runnels.

It's hard to believe that something so socially frightening could ever be psychically satisfying. Hard to believe that disease can bear gifts, can bring healing.

But we've always taken our prize family jewel for granted: the belief that life is meaningful.

"Life is real! Life is earnest! And the grave is not its goal; Dust thou art to dust returnest was not spoken of the soul." This bit of Longfellow was one of Mom's favorite and most frequent quotes, something we swallowed with peas.

Around that dinner table we were trained to seek, define, declare, appreciate, and create meaning.

(Whether life is actually meaningful is immaterial. Behaving as if it is, as if people and actions and experience matter, performs psychological alchemy.)

So we were inclined to regard Mom's decline as meaningful, which revealed its gifts, as thawing permafrost reveals patterns of heaved rock.

•••

For all my serious study of Zen, Alzheimer's is a living handbook: be present in the moment, accept without judgment things as they are, relieve suffering whenever possible, and practice nonattachment to any outcome.

Her diagnosis itself brings effortless detachment.

"Since Mom's no longer responsible for her behavior," I think with a lifting heart, "I can let go of any and all expectations. She can never disappoint me again, nor I her. We're finished hurting one another."

Clean slate. Sweet relief. Often only death brings such salve, but Mom's still alive. Freed of need and resentment, I can visit her. I can help ease her journey and lighten Ro's burden.

Rather than view the process of Mom's disease as random tangles webbing up her works, in our weekly phone calls Ro and I choose to see her symptoms through more creative lenses.

"If you'd grown up like Mom, with Gobby and Aunt Irene's inhibitions needlepointed into you, wouldn't it be a huge relief to actually scream and stamp and swing the range of feelings you'd contained for seventy years?"

"Yeah. No wonder they all loved the theatre—passions writ large and acted out loosened their emotional corsets for a few hours."

"That's probably why Mom threw the glass of water at me. And that slap I don't remember. I was emotional, demonstrative—"

"You still are."

"Ha, ha. If she wouldn't hear me, I at least wanted a genuine emotional reaction from her. Which was exactly how she was taught *not* to behave. But now she *gets* to. That has to be healthy, for her body at least."

•••

Since we have no earthly idea what is going on in her consciousness, we love speculating the wildest things.

"What if we're blobs of light to her, or auras? The whole air could be full of colored forms. Maybe she sees furniture as blocks of concentrated energy."

For a while Mom is obsessed with numbers, searching for sequences on the clock, the coded door.

"Maybe she's trying to figure a way out."

"Oooh, yeah—maybe she's peering between lifetimes."

"Maybe it's her Purgatory. The place she expected between here and Heaven."

The truth of such musings is not important, just the exercise.

•••

I visit when I can. It's not without pain, nor without laughter.

Sad to see this crossword champ flailing for words. Grievous her utter shock and sorrow when she understands at last she has Alzheimer's. Bitter-funny the day she grouses, "This disease is driving me crazy."

Her tantrums subside. Like a slow orchestral modulation from minor to major key, a new Betty emerges.

I meet her over coffee one morning. Out of nowhere:

"I'm proud of you and your book," she declares. "I'm showing it to people here. It's wonderful what you've done."

My jaw drops. Some months before, I'd sent her a copy of my first published book, about my weight struggles. I didn't expect to hear from her.

And now, astounding. And astoundingly gratifying.

"Gee—thanks, Mom."

She hugs me. Unbelievable.

"I love you." Can this be?

"I love you, too, Mom."

The glacier is melting, the pools by turns murky and crystalline.

•••

She's losing detail, memory, names, but we've never seen her happier—affectionate, demonstrative, openly loving. She's telling all the family members that she loves us. She hugs us, strokes our hands.

•••

Released from twenty years of massive sorrow carried since Dad's death, she's keeping company with Jack, a fellow resident who shares the name of her favorite childhood friend.

Ro phones for her one afternoon. "You might want to call back," says the nurse. "She and Jack are walking up and down the hall hand-in-hand."

•••

Of course the movements vary in her symphony of illness. There are sad, knee-weakening passages. Watching her shave her face with an electric razor. The queasy oddness of changing her Depends. The poignance of evaporating memory itself will pale in the late stage when she forgets how to swallow.

We try to ride the switching tides of time she surfs, through age and youth and foreign corridors of meaning. She's late for a college class, up with a colicky baby. Giggles, consternation, maybe now she's talking to Gobby? Official consciousness, official clock, official family history—no need for such frustration. Just expect the unpredictable.

•••

Midway through her process, I come for a week. One morning:

"I brought your favorite coffee cake, Mom."

"Oh, goody!" A hug and a kiss. Little things tickle her so.

We smile and munch. Quite a while. She yawns.

"I'll make you yawn again, " I say playfully and make up a sentence: "The awning salesman pawned the fawn upon the lawn." She yawns again, and so do I.

She laughs, I laugh, until we're collapsing with laughter. After the gale subsides, she looks me in the eye and says, with perfect lucidity, "You chose me."

Goosebumps. "I know, Mom. I'm glad. I learned a lot."

I'd never told her my belief that on some level we do choose
our parents, for reasons of our own. To hear this from her was
an imprimatur.

Then, with utter clarity and self-possession: "I had a big bad role,
didn't I?"

A shiver. "Yes," I say, "but it's over now."

We munch a little more.

"But thank you for saying it, Mom."

I open the poetry book I've brought and read her an old favorite:
The Owl and The Pussycat, ending with:

> *"And hand-in-hand, on the edge of the sand,*
> *They danced by the light of the moon,*
> *the moon,*
> *the moon,*
> *they danced by the light of the moon."*

"I haven't danced in so long," she sighs. I stand, hold out my arm.
"May I have this dance?"

Her eyes sparkle. She nods. I help her frail self up, sing a song of
sixpence, and almost imperceptibly, we dance.

•••

Eventually, dementia unravels all her sentences. When I visit, we
push a toy car back and forth. It's peaceful.

Mysteriously, when words are gone, song abides. Mom comes
'round the mountain and works on the railroad, never missing a beat, a
note, a lyric, though when the music stops she cannot speak a word.

Her decline is rapid—five years. When it's time, I fly back to help
her to hospice. Subtract her objects to a table, a bed, and the old crucifix.
This room, this thin room. This thinning deep-eyed face. Those feet
slipping under the sheet—I'll never see them again.

•••

In 1995, I concoct "Stand-Up Dreams," a performance based on twelve years of my dream journals. I book a little New York theater for the night of June 23rd to try it out.

The evening of June 22nd, Ro phones. "Mom's gone. John and I were there."

After the call, I pace our road, bathed in peach sunset light, but freezing. Freezing. June and I'm freezing, for blood recoils to the inwardest organs when the mother who bore you dies. No matter what the psyche has endured, the body will reverberate her death.

•••

Once again, in eerie parallel, my siblings say, "Go on with your show. Fly out on Sunday. We won't get there till then anyway." Once again, I do.

•••

In a few days, all seven of us gather for her service. We read Emily Dickinson and sing in harmony arm in arm again.

Ro, my husband, and I accompany her body to Minneapolis to be buried with Dad. We read a little something graveside, burn a big fat smudge stick like a mammoth cigarette, and think of how she gathered us together again, how helping her helped us.

Montana, Day Six: Inclinations

The cold rain streams over our sopping heads, our wincing faces, our knotted shoulders. But just as the gelid river water reaches our collarbones, the rock floor beneath us starts slanting upwards; incrementally, sluggishly, but definitely upwards.

We round the far side of the promontory. There, up the hill, is the glowing campsite.

One foot after another, muddy but unbowed. Through an icy stream with dammed-up side pool in which bob several cans of beer. Up, up the steep incline to be met at the top by the most welcome and staggering cliché: a cowboy in a white hat.

"Howdy! Name's Martin Hayes!" His eyes twinkle; his firm and friendly handshake pulls us toward the fire.

"Come on in, you look about half-drowned. Now I gotta warn you, there're some folks back there been drinkin', but they won't give you a hard time. They're really a friendly bunch. Want some coffee? Come over, get warm by the fire. Come in, come in, we're just fixin' to eat and we've got a whole lot. Got some ribs goin' now, havin' ribeyes later—we got plenty. Stay for dinner."

Thus begins our extraordinary evening.

"I'm going to go back and help our guys set up camp," says Don. In a flash he's gone, by way of an inland trail the cowboys point out above the promontory. No more clambering over the menacing rocks, even on our way back in the dark.

•••

The wilderness is the edge of so much: the edge of convenience, the edge of comfort, the edge of exertion, but not the edge of civilization. Not here. The rougher things get, the kinder people get.

Hot coffee, warm fire, fellowship. Living beatitudes. Giving food to the hungry.

Bobbing over to the fire are practically the first women we've seen on the trip—four or five of them. One offers me the fleece off her back—"You're soaked to the skin."

Which is literally true. But I say, "Thanks, but that's okay—I don't want you to get cold."

"Wanna glassa red wine?"

"Sure!" The coffee had taken the edge off.

"Have a rib!"

Vegetarian Ro passes, but I accept.

"Why'nch'a all stay for dinner? We have loads."

"Thanks so much, but our guy Mike is making his special chicken and dumplings tonight. He's been looking forward to it all trip. We need to be there."

"Got enough for them, too."

"You're terrific, but we'll head back soon. It's great to meet up with some women back here. How come we didn't see you on the river?"

"We come the other direction."

Rather than taking our route from Holland Lake, they'd brought their horses and gear in from the other end, along the Meadow Creek trail. They passed the spot where, day after tomorrow, we hope to hoist our rafts out of the water for good, leave our gear for the mules, pick up the Meadow Creek trail, and hike the last three and a half miles to the trailhead where Jim's friend Seidlitz—*where the heck is he?!*—has supposedly parked Jim's car with the promised cooler of ice-cold beer.

After we get over the Red Rapids, that is. Which after this rain will be flushing and gushing over the rocks.

Don't think about it. Feel how good it is to be warm, comforted with wine and warm people.

"Just came for the weekend. We been comin' for years. Martin's pal Guy used to own an outfitters. We only live in Missoula. Just come whenever we want."

Everyone's upwards of forty. They'd packed in enough supplies for an army, though they were just going tubing—no paddles—in flimsy-looking things that seem doppelgangers of children's wading pools.

Sharon, who had offered her golden fleece, says casually, "I nearly drowned today, going over that set of rapids, just yonder."

The deadly, red-rimmed "Scout These" rapids devilish whirling mess awaiting us day after tomorrow on our final rafting day.

"Yeah, I've summitted Rainier and I love all that adrenaline stuff, but them rapids almost took me—I was going over in the tube and I flipped out and I was underwater for the longest time, but I just kept thinking my brother'll get me, Martin'll get me, and he did. Leaped in and got hold of me and pulled me out. Tomorrow I'll be wearing my life jacket."

Hard to understand these people. Why no life jacket?

"Won't you stay for dinner?"

We just want to get back now and relax absolutely. Sleep. Weary.

"Thanks so much—we gotta get back. We should help them set up camp and then rest up. We have to take those rapids ourselves day after tomorrow."

"Keep to the left goin'—if you miss that you're in for trouble."

She. Nearly. Drowned.

After warm thanks and farewells, Ro and I wend our way down the crooked hill, past the little dam of cold beer, splash fast through the icy stream, and trudge up the long hill to the trail that leads to our campsite. It's nearly dark. The trail's mucky with rain, but at least it's not the deadly rocks.

Fifteen minutes more in the drenching downpour. When we are nearly to the site, here come Mike and Jack and Jim and Don and everybody lugging their stuff toward us.

"Turn around and go back," says Mike. "We can't make a campsite—there's no firewood, it's all rock. We'll have to spend the night with those folks."

"I think they'll be okay with that," I say. "Their tarp is enormous, and they have tents, too. Lots of food. They've been very friendly."

"Let's hope so."

Ro and I wearily pivot and slog back with the gang to Martin's camp.

They're surprised but happy to see us.

"We got tons of food—come on in!"

Logistics first. The men and women haul all their stuff to one end of the giant tarp so we can pile ours in. Our intrepid guys go out in the pelting rain and pitch Big Agnes for us. And they brought us dry clothes.

"You can change here," says Sharon, pointing to a spacious stand-up-in-able tent. We practically trip in anticipation. Soon, after eight hours of being cold and wet, we revel in the simple animal comfort of being warm and dry.

The gents flip ribeyes on the grill; Ro and I help the women set out bread, cheese, salad, and three versions of homemade huckleberry pie. Don wins everyone's gratitude again, for their water filter is sluggish. He hooks up our specially rigged one, so there's plenty of water with little waiting.

As Ro compares notes with a retired first grade teacher, Sharon tells me about life on her ranch.

"Lucky I live next to a veterinarian, 'cause last month when my gate swung back and gashed my head? I could call her to come stitch me up. Turns out I didn't need 'em."

She lifts her black bangs revealing a nasty but healing red furrow.

"So close here, 'cross my forehead into my scalp. She said I'd be fine without. Tough to stitch the scalp, you know." One tough woman.

Good food, big laughter, great stories, human tribal joy. Finding that hospitality means not only entertaining angels unaware, but being cared for by them yourself.

After we've eaten our fill, Mike draws me aside.

"We thought we should have your special Scotch tonight. With our hosts."

He's referring to the gift I planned to give Jim on our last night—the most extravagant bottle I have ever bought.

How thoughtful Mike is. "Absolutely," I say. "What a great idea. Sorry Jim won't get as much as I hoped, but it's the perfect gesture of thanks."

Round go the red Solo cups. Nine of us, twelve of them. A ceremonial taste for all.

Like a priest of the wilderness, Jim tips elixir into each cup while I tell the story of this Scotch.

"Jim heard about Bruichladdich, and decided, taste untasted, to buy a bottle. He *still* hasn't tasted it. He keeps telling us that he's set it aside for his wake.

"So I secretly had a bottle sent to Mike, who packed it in. It's twenty-two years old and called Black Art, and you could buy a decent pair of boots for what it cost. But it seems to me a man who loves and appreciates good single malt shouldn't have to wait until he's dead to taste it. I was gonna surprise him on our last night, but this is the ideal occasion. We're honored to share it with all you generous, extraordinary folk."

We all toast each other and sip the liquid marvel.

"Mmmm," they say. "This Funeral Scotch is good."

•••

I take another sip then give Jim the rest. After all, it was for him. Time for bed, or rather, for bag.

Ro and I repair to our tent, our hosts to theirs. Their pack drivers camp further off. Our guys and Lauren shelter under the giant tarp as buckets of rain stream down, closing a day exhausting and exhilarating in each extreme.

Wills Read and Written

The last time all we siblings are together is for The Reading of the Will.

Not Mom's.

Tom gathers us all in a hotel room to carry out the duty he assumed. Even John manages to make it.

•••

What long roots of family love, you have, Tom, reaching back to the family tree you drew on the fold-down desk you built. Most practical of us all, you know your way around a toolbox and a contract and half the airports in the world. But you know your way around the human heart as well, and spring to spare it pain.

After Dad died, even as you reared your two fine sons, you and Linda kept an eye on Mom, took her on trips, talked with her. You and Linda traveled, too, with lonely Mary Kay and Mom's unmarried sister Ellen, an executive secretary. Did odd jobs for them, helped them move. Gave them bountiful gifts of time, of love, of attention we could not. Gallant, in the best old-fashioned rescuing-a-girl-and-her-schoolbook-from-the-icy-creek sense.

•••

So when we fly in for the funeral and gather in the hotel room, it is because you have performed the myriad tasks of executor.

Of course, there are not enough chairs for all of us—we are scattered over beds, couch, and floor. With a smile, you announce that Aunt Ellen was well-paid, thrifty, and an excellent investor. She wanted all us here together to discover, as you read, that she was leaving her charming Culver City bungalow to Mary Kay and that each of us will receive several thousand dollars from her substantial estate. We're staggered, laughing, slapping our foreheads. Who'da thunk it? I make a joke that makes Pogo laugh—a treasure nugget, for though he is not speaking to me, it cheers me still to make him laugh.

It is just at this moment, as I sit on the floor at Mary Kay's knee, that I catch the first whiff of Mary Kay's decline. Unmistakable. She is incontinent.

•••

Later we Youngers see the heartbreaking state of her house. It's the bungalow Ellen left her, which she and Ellen neatly shared for years. Kako has lived here alone since Ellen moved to assisted living three years ago.

Thirty unopened QVC boxes obstruct her porch. Inside, she's hoarding, living with dirt, rotting food, trash, not even letting her little dogs outside to relieve themselves. It's clear her mind is slipping and that she can't care for herself. Her deterioration is especially hard on Tom and Linda, for while Kako's been distant from us, she's Tom's Big Sis, Linda's friend, and like a grandma to their boys. I can't imagine how I'd feel were I watching Ro decline like this.

Jim and I confer. That night at dinner, we tell our siblings he and I will take responsibility for Mary Kay.

"Ro took care of Mom; Tom and Linda watched over Ellen and Kako. It's our turn to step up to the plate."

A warm wash of gratitude from those who have already served.

•••

Jim's expertise proves hugely helpful; his emotional support indispensable as we navigate the vagaries of the medical system and the legal system on behalf of Mary Kay and *her* disintegrating system.

I'm on the phone with him now much more often; we take trips to California to handle the multitude of necessities, from getting Mary Kay diagnosed, (yes, early Alzheimer's) to helping her make a will and arranging Power of Attorney. Although impaired, she has enough smarts to know what she's doing and tells us she knows we have her best interest at heart. Jim and I share meals, martinis, laughter, and angst. On these trips I also spend more time with Tom and Linda and their kids, some of whom come to help clean out the house. Ro flies down when she can and is especially helpful when we need to move Kako to assisted living.

•••

And you, dear Kako, distant sister, independent woman of granite resolve these many years, I've gotten to know you and your history as both are dissolving. Like Mom, you bestow the Zen privilege of loving you now in the moment however you need. I'm grateful to thank you for mothering me in my earliest days by mothering you in your last ones.

And suddenly, I see our gift to you has returned to us a family-fold, for our efforts to be sure you live with human decency have brought most of us siblings closer than ever. Thanks to you, we've gotten to know each other better, to enjoy each other's company. We now make time, take trips with each other. Even into the wilderness.

Montana, Day Seven: Bequests

Next morning, as planned, our hosts prepare to depart. This superb campsite is ours for today and tonight; tomorrow we leave.

But first, we lend a hand with breakfast: stoke up the fire, grill massive amounts of smoky bacon, scramble a few dozen eggs, and toast stacks of English muffins.

After eats and cleanup, Martinsquats on his bootheels, stuffing barware into a nylon sack. He tips his white straw Stetson back and looks Jim in the eye.

"You live in Missoula, too, don'cha Jim??"

"That I do, Martin. That I do."

"Well, why don't we just leave our table and propane stove for ya? You can bring it to us when you get back. And take all this food we brought. We're just going home."

There's a stomach-boggling amount: big industrial packs of cold cuts, cheeses, mustard, mayo. Package upon package of sliced bread. Loads of fresh fruit: cantaloupe, apples, oranges. A knee-high carton of granola bars. Candy. Musta been one wild trip to Costco.

"Martin, that's so generous, but we're only here one more day ourselves—"

"Nonsense. Take and have."

His beefy friend Guy is poking through grocery bags. He holds up a green net sack.

"Here's them Key limes we brought for drinks! Looked all over for 'em!" He tosses them back in the bag. "Well, you folks enjoy."

He's opening tubs and sniffing. "Whooo. Some stuff went bad."

He carries the offenders—yogurt, sour cream, guacamole— and blops them directly on the campfire. Still in their containers. Dumbfounded, I dart upwind of the heap of burning plastic.

They do things differently in Montana. When I later look it up, though, I find that "the destruction of combustible material by burning" is not prohibited in The Bob.

And Don and Jack will later shock Ro and me by pulling down the gigantic plastic tarp and making a huge smelly smoldering bonfire of it. Weren't gonna pack it out, I guess.

But how can we hold anything against these kind people who've been so good to us? Who offered warmth and shelter and food and wine and lively company?

Jim gets their Missoula number and address, a group photo is snapped, we hug and wish each other well. The riders mount up and head out on the trail.

Martin and Sharon, though, board their tubes at the water's edge and shove off. Waving goodbye with wide toothy smiles, twirling and swooping in the swollen river, they want another trip down the middle of her near-death experience. I don't want to watch them, but I do, through my fingers. They emerge hooting and spinning and grinning downriver.

The Red Rapids. Some people make it through.

•••

Things quiet down. Our final day in camp.

We've been talking quietly for a while when somebody spots a red-haired man in the river. He's in his thirties, well-built, bearing a towering backpack, trying to cross the wide and swiftly moving river at a deep point nerve-wrackingly close to the Red Rapids.

We call and motion to him. "Don't ford there! Come back this way! It's easier!"

But he proceeds—doesn't seem to get it.

"Can we string a rope to him?" I ask.

We scramble for lengths, tie them together and toss it to him, but he doesn't use it. It's only then we notice the string of eight skinny boy backpackers gathering on the opposite bank.

Don coils the rope back in and heads toward the horse trail. What's he up to?

As the man reaches shore, Don gallops down with one of the last beers from the cooling dam. He offers it to the man, who refuses.

"Thanks. Can't do that now."

This ginger hunk of muscle introduces himself as Alton.

"I'm on duty. These teens are part of a program for troubled youth. Each one's had difficult personal experiences, and The Bob helps them become self-reliant. It's why we can't use a rope. They have to cross on their own. We've been back for three weeks, clearing and repairing trails for the forest service. And folks like you."

"Well, thanks," we say. Alton chuckles and peers back at the river.

Choosing a slightly shallower ford, he wades back to the boys and lines them up at the lower end of the rapids, just above the treacherous place.

One by one, they make it to our shore.

"Can't we give them some granola bars?" Lauren asks.

She flies up the hill and brings down the knee-high box.

Hungry as they are, they must wait for permission from Alton, who is helping his co-captain over. Jake's having a difficult time.

When at last they stumble onto shore, Alton gives the granola go-ahead.

The ravenous boys rip into the sweet snacks.

Suddenly we realize how much food is left—ham, cheese, bread.

"Come up, come up and get something real to eat!"

Less than twenty-four hours earlier, we'd received unbelievable bounty. That was joyful, but more joy to bestow it right away, to see these half-starved teenagers wolf down vast quantities of ham, cheese, bread, canned peaches, applesauce. They squeal when they see the fresh fruit—cantaloupes, apples, oranges. For weeks they've lived mostly on ramen and pasta.

When we pull out the leftover huckleberry-raspberry pies, they nearly weep.

They are as grateful as we were last night.

We pull out the Story Tarp, which is now covered with sharpie-ed images of our trip. To a man, they sign it.

When it's time, we bid them farewell. Off they march in glee and vigor, following the very trail taken by our benefactors a few scant hours ago.

•••

The afternoon unfolds in peace and quiet. Jim and Ro reteach me cribbage. We play awhile, a friendly game. They're kind to the rookie.

Jim unfolds himself from the camp chair, takes up the sole remaining fly rod, saunters down to the beach, makes a few casts.

For the last several days, in his big chef's cooler Mike has secretly transported turkey, cranberry sauce, and Stove Top stuffing over the river and through the woods. He's planned a campfire Thanksgiving. As he readies the fire and his cauldrons, I chop onions, my eyes already moist.

The last of the scotch is gone, but I remember the twelve Key limes. Our hosts also left us sugar. Hmmm. I look around. There's still some un-"num-nummed" vodka. Ro and I make simple syrup over the fire, squeeze every drop from the limes, and mix delicious vodka gimlets for cocktail hour.

The young ones amuse themselves building their own little campfire.

It's a delicious, profound August Thanksgiving, bellies full of turkey, faces sticky with s'mores. I produce the wax lips and mustaches my husband sent with me for a photo op. What the picture captures is the spirit of the child still living in Lauren, Derek, Dominic, and Uncle Jack.

"Hey, where's Seidlitz?" asks Jack suddenly.

"Don't know," says Jim. 'But I know him. He'll be here."

We review the Story Tarp. Jim fishes deep into sunset.

And for once Ro and I can completely relax, because Jack and Mike gave us a touching gift that brims our eyes with relief: earlier in the day, without our knowledge, they rode one of the rafts over the dangerous rapids. Tomorrow morning they'll take the other over it. Ro and I can skip the fearsome Red Rapids altogether and walk the trail, meeting them on shore beyond. There we'll load both rafts and take the last five miles more leisurely. We might even float.

Thanksgiving 2013

In 2013, Ro and her husband Mark move into their charming forties bungalow. Wanting a big family Thanksgiving, they invite Mark's Dad, their sons, brothers John and Jim, and me and my husband. Ro's sons will be there, too. We don't travel at the holidays, but we make an exception this year.

I'm eager to see everyone, to see what Ro's done with the place, to see her new artwork. She's now developed her art in multiple ways: she draws and paints, sews, knits, dyes, and felts. In this house she has her own studio for the first time. She's writing, too.

And of course, it's plain grand to see her. We'll cook side by side, sing in harmony, and laugh our ages off. Share intimate fulfilling conversations.

We mother each other, healing our daughterhood.

•••

Among your gifts, Ro, acts of deep witness. Not only yours to me, but mine to you. Bedside as you labor and deliver your first child, I choke with tears and laughter as the little head emerges, struck with a kinetic comprehension of our mother, our womanhood, and our humanity at once.

I've subsequently grasped from you the sheer relentless physicality of parenting and its relentless emotional upheaval. Yet how your love outdistances exhaustion and resentment. You've proved it can be done, and artfully.

Ro's kitchen is elegant, but compact. Preparing Thanksgiving dinner calls for shifting, sensitive choreography. Though we would have clobbered each other as children, these subtle movements of respect are a pleasure for us all.

After a wonderful meal and a spirited bridge game, Mark leaves to drive his father back to the hotel. Brother John bids us a warm farewell and limps to his car for his long drive home.

"Too bad he has such a long drive. Why did he move thirty miles out of town?"

"He never told us. We haven't been there—he hasn't invited us yet."

Ro and Mark keep an eye on John. For years he was able to eke out a living as a classical guitarist, performing and giving guitar lessons. He asked our help in financing a CD, which he sold at gigs, but it's Ro and Mark who have consistently made sure he's solvent and celebrated. He always has a place at their table for holidays, birthdays, and the occasional bridge game. They paid him to give music lessons to their children. As time went on and there were fewer gigs for classical guitarists and fewer students, Mark gave him a job in his law office, so at least he's had an income for fourteen years. They also took him in for several weeks and nursed him back to health while he recovered from diabetic shock.

"He seemed pretty good tonight, but I'm surprised he didn't bring his guitar."

"Yeah he hasn't brought it the last few times."

"Well, *I* brought something," says Orion, Ro's older son. Out of a backpack he pulls a baby food jar of marijuana. We laugh. We siblings haven't smoked individually in ages nor together in several decades. But Washington has just passed a law. He rolls a joint and offers it to us. The first legal smoke of our lives.

We puff, move to the living room, group around the handsome fire Mark built, and enjoy several stages of stoned: giggling, reminiscing, sighing into silence. Layers of love intensified.

Like young twin wizards, Ro's boys slouch in black hoodies and jeans, by turns bemused, inquisitive, observant, hilarious, blowing perfect smoke rings as we remember the things we always remember, our landscape's well-worn paths: the stinky-sponged dish arguments, the stinky laundry room, the stink of the green sunroom chairs, the stink of us. The house smelling like a den of young animals. Which it was.

Remembering infinitesimal domesticities: the rhythm of the upstairs faucet, the specific squeak of the corner cupboard door, the bark on the second-base oak in the back.

Giving each other hard times for the hard times we gave each other—

"You so lorded it over Jim and me," Ro says. "Had to be priest when we played Mass, and we had to crucify you for Holy Week."

"Because I could never be an altar boy. Jim had real authority"

She rightfully grouses about the time Mom asked her to clean the fireplace.

"I didn't want to do it. Irene said she would if I'd do her 'infinity' favors."

"You didn't know what infinity meant, right?" asks Jim.

"I becked and called her for years," I admit. "And I apologize again for my twenty-third birthday, Ro."

"What happened?" asks her younger son.

"It was her 'golden' birthday," says Ro. "Because she was born on the twenty-third day of the month, I gave her twenty-three presents. She opened them and then promptly went out with her friends. Didn't even invite me. I cried and cried. Then Jim said, 'You just have to take Irene as she is.'"

I swell with gratitude for these two siblings. I bore no children. I thought I'd put a stop to family patterns, spare myself the sight of pain, scribbled on a child's face, authored by me. I didn't want a lifetime of guilt after a lifetime of guilt. I also thought I'd spare myself the bother of loving those who may or may not love me back. Looking at my various siblings, I see I've done both in spite of myself.

"You both know me at my worst. Thanks for loving me anyway."

More old stories tumble out. They recall a showdown I've forgotten:

Dad insists I eat the liver and onions which he loves and on which I gag. I cannot.

"You will sit at the table until you do."

I *cannot* swallow it. Hours later, he lets me leave, though without any dinner.

"We were impressed," Jim says.

We twist again the puzzle of Mom.

"How she hated maintenance."

"Maintenance, like olives, is an acquired taste. The older I get the more I like it."

"And they didn't have yoga, exercise, therapy, or meditation much back then. Martinis, paperbacks, and Confession were pretty much it for stress relief."

We laugh anew at one of her particular duplicities:

After Mom had sufficiently recovered from her brain operation, it was time for me to fly back to New York. As I was packing, she came in and said, "Thank you, dear, for all your help. You know, you remind me more of your father than anyone else in the family."

Wow. The highest possible compliment. I carried her words with a secret glow of pride until one night years later when we Youngers were talking family. I finally worked up the courage to confess she'd so anointed me.

Ro and Jim both gasped and said in unison: "She told me *I* was the one that most reminded her of Dad!" After the initial pinch, we scream with laughter. Tricked again.

But she did write letters that fizz with our youth. I share a few tidbits that night:

" 'Ro said we're having "Chork Pops" for dinner.' Jimmie wants to 'stand on the bathroom camera that tells how many numbers we are.' "

And my favorite—"Jim and Ro have lots of fun together ...the other day he came up to her playpen singing (to the tune of Little Brown Jug) 'Ha, ha, ha, you and me; Little Ground Hog, how I love thee.' "

•••

Comfortable silence falls again.

•••

We talk about the confidence they've instilled in their own children, the sense of joy, the love of their bodies and of physicality, along with the positives we got. Jewels among the sand, the silt, the sludge:

"Sure we never learned how to do laundry, or paperwork, or mail a package, keep a house clean, but that you can learn."

"Especially if you marry someone who knows how, the way most of us did!"

"But we did get senses of humor, of meaning, of justice. Love of spirit, of language, of meaning. Faith. We listen to people. We make good friends. We suffered each other and were suffered. Sanded off each other's rough edges."

"And their marriage was a good enough model for most of us."

Another wave of silence.

"How is everyone?" Ro asks.

"That question is Capsule Ro," I say, writing in my little blue notebook. Grass makes me want to write down all my thoughts.

"Is there a phrase you'd say captures you?" I ask Jim.

"Whatever my answer is, it's going to be in that notebook." Which is Capsule Jim—always trying to anticipate and outthink.

Later he offers an alternative: "I am always learning."

A few more Capsule Ro's:

"I want my laugh."

"Don't blame me."

"May I sing?"

Every night before she went to bed, Ro asked Mom and Dad, "May I sing?" Not to us, but to herself, as she fell asleep. She was always granted permission.

Tonight we ask at last, "What *were* you singing about?"

"The family," she answers. Of course. "Oh, Mary Kay is a nun, and Tom is at college...I was trying to keep everybody straight."

Youthful Capsule Irene was, "I'm offering it up," but I let that go early, telling Mom one day, "I was going to offer up my itch, but then I thought what would the angels do with an itch?" Now Capsule Irene is: "Here's a question."

Capsule us? "That Went Fast."

We marvel anew at the bonging grandmother clock the night Dad died. Pogo has the clock, but, sadly, not nights like this.

Wordlessly, in perfect concord, we imbibe the familiar flow of each other's presence. The embers topple, glow. Bing's "White Christmas" plays softly in the background. Unbeknownst to us, next summer, we'll entrust our lives to one another in the wilderness.

Piecing Together

A few months later, I leave a message on John's phone, wishing him a happy birthday.

For all the angst and awkwardness I often felt with him, for all his arguments and pontificating and sense of entitlement, he's mellowed with the years.

Whenever I called Ro at a holiday, she'd ask if I wanted to talk with him. During our guarded conversations, we noticed striking parallels—"I'm growing bonsai," he said once.

"Me, too!" I answered.

Another time we discovered he was studying Buddhism as I accelerated my exploration of Zen.

We were able to talk about the challenges of being artists, and when I came to see Ro, he and I enjoyed some peaceful visits to the Portland Japanese Garden. I mellowed, too, thanks to a spontaneous choice in an airport bookstore.

In 2006, looking for an airplane read, I grabbed *Born On Blue Day* by Daniel Tammet—a memoir describing his personal experience of Asperger Syndrome, a disorder now considered part of the autism spectrum.

Social difficulties, lack of empathy, lack of eye contact, verbosity, obsession with a narrow area of interest, difficulty with self-care, excessive blinking, catatonia. My God. That's what's wrong with John. This has a name. Nowadays it is easy to see that what felt like selfishness, hypocrisy, and disregard was a disorder. So easy to see now, so hellish to live through.

Afraid of his possible response, it's some years before I gently broach the subject with him.

But at tea one afternoon, after the Japanese Garden:

"I read an interesting Asperger book, John."

Some discussion, then "Do you think...?"

"I've wondered that myself," he says, and moves on to other topics.

We couldn't talk about this, but we could be gentler with
one another.

•••

He doesn't return my birthday call—I'm not surprised, but when
Ro's call to him goes unacknowledged, she keeps calling for a few days.
"Please call me back. We want to celebrate your birthday. I'm getting
worried about you."

He doesn't call. Ro and Mark have never been to his place—he's
never invited them. But they drive the thirty miles and track it down: a
tiny one-bedroom attached unit in a small row of five.

They knock, then bang. Still no response. Mark punches 911 into his
phone. When the police and paramedics arrive, Mark enters with them
and finds John's body in bed.

"He was dressed for bed," Mark later told me. "And he had a look of
wonder on his face."

Dying in his bed, a comfort. His living space, a horror.

Though Mark and son Orion spent the next day clearing it and Ro
joined them the following day, their efforts will be impossible to detect
when I at last arrive, so colossal is the chaos.

Others in our family expressed depression through household
neglect, through filth and heaps and hoards, whether it was Mary Kay's
slide into Alzheimer's and the shared experience of clearing out her
heartbreaking place, or that shocking visit to Mom's apartment after
her medical emergency. Even Jim, a widower living with his bachelor
sons, needed to be freed of soul-crushing debris when he sold their
house. The only way to keep from breaking apart as I did this work
was to continually say, "This is so beautiful. This is so very beautiful,"
as tears streamed down. And there *is* something beautiful in being
trusted with such ugliness, in being allowed to express love by helping to
transform it.

Ro cleaned these anguished spaces with me.

"John's is worse," she warns. "No wonder he never invited us. It's just mountains of trash. But Mark and Orion found four musical instruments buried under papers, garbage, rotting clothes."

"What about his guitar?" His finest, his most beloved, treasured object: the superb instrument he had saved up to buy and which he played for years: a classical guitar commissioned by master guitarist Julian Bream.

"Hanging on the wall, covered in dust. With a broken string."

Pierced my heart to hear it. His chief pleasure gave him no pleasure. Bone and blood is the price of coal.

"Not only that. We found dozens of candles, Coleman stove gas, a camo vest, canned food. He was a *survivalist*. And this heavy locked box. He always told Mom to invest in gold bullion, but when we opened it—Oh, Ree," she wails.

A revolver and multiple rounds of ammunition.

My peace activist brother, the conscientious objector, lived with unfathomed fear and dread. Paranoia, also characteristic of Asperger's.

•••

Ro feels I should wait a day before going to his house, so together we tend the thousand details death occasions: writing the obituary, creating the service, finding the funeral home and a place for a post-memorial reception, ordering food, notifying anyone she could remember. She met the grueling challenge of his cremation before I got there.

And everything cost money we'll never see again. Ka-ching, ka-ching, ka-ching. Bitter shameful thought: he always expects the cash outlay, even now. But there's such a thing as human decency.

Late that afternoon, Ro leaves to get Mark at his office.

Alone, I lay on the couch, dreading having to clear out yet another abhorrent malodorous dwelling. Why is this our family signature, I fume. I want to mourn John, not resent him for what he left me to mop up. Do I even have the emotional fortitude to face this? Welcome to the mouth of hell.

It's not fair. Why do I even have to? What do people who don't have siblings do? Who cleans up after *them*?

Whatever I do, it's never enough. Money was never enough. Concern or questions or gifts were never enough. He couldn't forgive me for not visiting him in the looney bin.

But if I had gone, what might he have done? Hit me, perhaps. Scalded me with words, surely. His anger was terrifying; his skill in humiliation, unmatched. Whatever the outcome, I wouldn't feel better for seeing him. Nor would he.

Tears slide. Always feared him. Never felt it so starkly. Shouldn't be afraid of your own brother. Especially now you know he was impaired. But I was afraid, always.

I suddenly grasped this brutal totality. No wonder he was hard to be around. I was always on the defensive. And while I'd tried over the years to understand and forgive him, it never occurred to me to forgive myself. For being afraid.

At this, my guilt shattered like a mirror dropped.

I don't have to do this. I email my brother Tom.

"What do landlords do when people leave apartments in this condition?"

He'll know. He's a landlord himself. Cleanup may cost a bundle, but it'll be worth every penny.

•••

Ro and Mark return with unbelievable, magical news.

"The landlord liked John. He says we should take what we want and he'll take care of the rest. He'll clear away everything."

A miracle.

The next day I said to Ro, "So we're not cleaning up. We're going on a treasure hunt." (Albeit with latex gloves and filter masks.)

It was good we had that image of hope. The devastation and embodied despair of his apartment was almost more than I could bear. Darkest, filthiest, most wretched of human dwellings. The sight of his bathroom catapulted sobs out of me. "Oh, no! Oh, no, oh, no, oh, no."

That anyone should live here. That it was you, Skip.

No descriptions of the indescribable, just the treasures. Carvings from your trip to South America. Your cascade juniper bonsai, still well cared for. In addition to the musical instruments, Ro found a breathtaking appraisal of your guitar. When sold, it would cover funeral expenses and then some.

The real treasure, though, was finding out how many people genuinely liked you. Donating your books at the local library, we found your fellow volunteers were saddened by your death. Such a genial guy. Great jokes. We'll miss him.

Other folks had enjoyed hiking and camping with you. You'd even been part of a men's group. Who knew?

•••

Would your life have been different if there had been a diagnosis in your childhood? My teeth ache when I think of your loneliness and your fear.

You had an eyepatch over your social eye, and no one could see it, not even you. How painful not to share your life with someone.

Did people's actions puzzle you? Did you ever understand how frustrating you could be? Did this hurt, or did you not perceive it? Did you turn then to the guitar, to your books, to your movies, to your pipe when you smoked it, to your garden when you had one, did you just turn away and not ask?

It was a symptom of yours, thinking you didn't need help, a mean trick your disorder played, for you never really got it, except from Ro and her family.

When I listen to your CD, beneath your Villa-Lobos, your O'Carolan, I hear the very soundtrack of your feelings: your confidence, your pride, your pleasure in intricate fingering, delicate trills, thunderous punctuation, simple strumming. I feel your joy in mastery. I sense your hope, yielding to emotion in the music; your rare frustration with a tricky passage.

I think of the hours, the years of errors an acutely sensitive musician must tolerate to perform a concerto not just accurately, but beautifully. What self-forgiveness and patience he must practice along with the chords, devoting himself not just to technique, but to the highest expression possible. Once the sequences become second nature, he must trust himself to release all preparation and simply play.

Tolerance. Forgiveness. Patience. Devotion. Trust. Exactly what a well-played human life requires.

Listening more deeply, below even the soft chirp of your fingers over the frets, I detect one of the oldest sounds of my life: the familiar sound of your breathing. The music of yourself, audible beyond death.

Montana, Day Eight:
No Second Chance

Characteristic of this journey, just as Ro and I snugly relax in our sleeping bags, there's a muscle-clutching rumble of thunder. Brilliant flashes flicker Big Agnes like a zoetrope, and now buckets of rain slosh against her, wind pummels her, slugging our hearts in our chests. Such a thin small piece of cloth between us and this fierce storm. Fearsome booms echo around the mountain range. Please don't sop through and soak our sleeping bags—please not cold and wet like yesterday.

After a quivering, sleepless night, sunrise. We hightail it and pack up.

Jim and I pose for a photo with the empty Bruichladdich bottle. They burn the giant tarp—a sad demise for the gift of shelter.

Carrying as much as possible, Ro and I plod back down the muddy trail to meet up with everyone else on the other side of the Red Rapids for the last leg of our journey.

When we find them, the men are taking turns pumping up the leaky raft one last time. Then we shove off.

Quieter today, more mysterious. A moment or two to contemplate the miraculous. Kingfishers to cheer Ro. (Her totem.) Deeper glassier pools than any we have seen. Clarity through immense depth. This part is more float than paddle, and it is holy indeed.

The river is picking up speed, though. Suddenly we crash on an unforeseen rock with such force that Jim flies out of the raft into the rushing river. The look on his face is terrifying.

No, no. We're stuck on the rock and can't reach him. We jiggle, bounce, lurch, try everything to jolt ourselves loose so we can get to Jim before he's swept away. Thank God that today for some reason (Sharon?) he saw fit to put a lifejacket on. He has surfaced. He stands in chest-high water, ashen-faced, but upright and breathing. Our raft won't budge.

"We got you, Jim." shouts Ro.

"We don't have him," says Don.

"We're getting him. We'll get him!" snaps Ro, arms out, straining their sockets.

Jim staggers against the strong current with all his strength, reaching toward her with some hesitation. Don leans forward and grabs his arm. Together they re-raft him.

"I did what you're supposed to do when you fall in: let the equipment do its work. I relaxed and let the life jacket bring me back to a float. Then orient your feet downstream and stand if you can."

Nice of you to tell us the rules on the last day, Jim, Ro and I think simultaneously.

"Why didn't you grab my hand?" Ro asks.

"I saw your thin little arms and I didn't want to pull you in."

For all the scrapes and challenges and agitation and self-preservationary fear churned by this journey, the most stomach-sickening brunt to bear is the horror of watching people you love fall into dangerous waters.

People do die in front of each other.

The body's charged with joy each time they don't, but is that recompense enough?

As we manage at last to dislodge raft from rock, I have the heart-stopping thought that if we'd done so earlier, we would have rocketed right over Jim.

No time for relief—we're barreling toward another huge jagged tangle of brush. When will this be *over*?

I'm inwardly angry. I want to be relieved. I want to enjoy what's left of this trip, not resent it. But my emotions aren't my own. They belong to the river and what she offers. I can't help wanting it to be over. Emotions can't follow their own rhythm here. They supersede each other like the torrents we careen.

•••

There's supposed to be a big red-and-white sign marking the take-out point.

We've been repeatedly warned: we must not miss it. No rafts are allowed beyond the take-out point, and if you miss it, there's no second chance, because the river immediately breaks into extremely dangerous class 4 and 5 rapids. What's worse, there's no way to get off the river—no beaches, no shores, no stopping. Just sheer walls on either side of the twisty narrow channel. Even professional paddlers are rarely permitted here, much less three-day experts like Ro and me.

Oh, God, where's the sign? Will we make the sharp turn? Maybe they took the sign down. Paddle, paddle, scouring the hills, the trees for the red-and-white sign.

Derek spots a tiny black-and-white sign that says "take-out ahead," as if a greasy spoon were up around the bend.

"Pull! Pull! Over to the right—Get over! Get over!!"

Massive electrical effort. We can't believe we make the turn. But we do.

"Is this it? Is this really it?"

"Yup—aim for that rock beach there. We'll pull up and empty the rafts."

Unbelievable. We're there. We're here. It's over. We made it. We're all alive. I'm so relieved I nearly throw up.

Help pull up the raft.

I pick up a quarter-sized white stone to take with me, a reminder of my survival.

"Irene, you start carrying things up to the packers. We'll empty the raft."

Gently, walk gently over the twisty river rocks. Shaking with relief, you still have to be careful.

Up there, at last, the damn red-and-white sign: Dangerous Water Ahead Remove Boats Here.

A short three-minute trail leads from the take-out to the pack mule staging area. Another party's already there loading up, so I deliver dry bags, gear, boxes, the Papa Bear cast-iron cauldron to a small clearing below. Up and down, up and down. Earth is such comfort. At least I know what I'm doing.

My arms are full of paddles when I see a lanky, bespectacled form. John Seidlitz.

"Hi. Let me get those. Great to see you. Sorry I got delayed—Dad needed help. Figured I'd join you here rather than trying to find your campsite. Cars are waiting below, and the beer's on ice."

How do you spell relief?

The guys must deflate and fold the rafts so they can be put back on mules—an arduous task. A group of fly fishermen are headed out. Don enlists their help in exchange for a library of casting flies he's brought along. A man prepared for all contingencies.

The men are delighted to help—more evidence of backcountry courtesy and deal-brokering.

Our packers and mules will arrive in their own good time. We needn't wait, just start walking. How good to have our feet under us, how safe the trail feels, though it curves along a high precipice, which might have weak-kneed me before but can't faze me now. I survived this trip. I can do practically anything.

We look to the dangerous waters far below, the narrow scalloped passes any raft would be blasted into. No place to hide, to slow, to stop, to escape.

We are safe, we are together, we love each other, we've all done our best, we're proud, and uniquely bonded. It's touching to overhear Mike asking not Don, but Lauren, "How do you raise a girl?" He's nervous about the daughter he and Jolyne are expecting. "What do you suggest? I haven't been around girls that much."

"Just listen to her," Lauren advises. Wise kid.

The walk feels good, stretching our muscles, decompression time.

We yield to horses and mules on the trail—they have right of way.

Halfway down we meet a small procession coming up. Whoops of joy and recognition—our backpacker boys. As our line passes their line, we high-five the whole way.

We cross a bridge above a narrow green channel river-chiseled through the gray-faced rock. A sparkling, spectacular (tourist) vantage.

Down to the bathroom, the tailgate, the crisp brew waiting. Very delicious.

Every muscle quaking.

Finally we climb into the car for the three-hour drive through yet more scenic Montana landscape. Destination: the Hungry Horse, for legendary huckleberry milkshakes and cellphone service so spouses can learn all is well, we made it. Where we will learn that the GPS was impaired, that it only worked every few days, and had we been in trouble, it would not have dispatched help.

Rubber-legging thought. But now we're good at letting go of scary thoughts. These milkshakes are delicious. I buy huckleberry souvenirs for my husband.

Back to Seely Lake, where we camped that lifetime ago, for dinner with Jolyne, Creighton, and the baby girl to come.

They'll drive 130 miles back to Conrad tonight, so after dinner, we repack the trailer behind Mike's SUV. Jim will drive it back to Missoula with the U of M rafts, the table and stove left by our hosts, our packs and bags.

"Thanks for the trip of a lifetime, Ramrod." We hug them goodbye.

"Careful driving back," says Jolyne. "That stretch of road has a lot of deer at night."

"I'll follow them in Jim's Prius," Jack offers.

The dark landscape streams by. We're physically spent and all talked out.

Most of us have early flights in the morning. And we're as ravenous for hot showers as our backpackers for fruit.

At 11 p.m., just ten miles from Missoula, the SUV starts shaking.

"Jim," Ro says," I think we should pull over. Something's wrong."

"Naaah," he says. "It's just the load we're pulling. Steering gets a little funny, that's all."

"Jim, please."

We stop, take flashlights around the back.

One of the two trailer tires is shredded to the rim.

Ro nearly goes over the edge. "I knew something was wrong. Oh no."

I guide her back inside. "Just sit here and breathe. Everything will be all right."

Can't *believe* this isn't over yet. We're so close. Are a shower and some sheets and sleep too much to ask?

Happily, Jack and Don notice from the Prius and pull over.

Don works for AAA. He calls the local office. This will be solved.

"Jack, drive Irene and Ro and Lauren back to the hotel. We'll wait for Triple A. Things'll be okay."

Smells of woodsmoke as we enter Missoula. Orange light flickers in the hills.

"Talked with a friend," Jack says. "Twenty-three wildfires burning around Missoula. Started by lightning. That same storm."

Same storm that rattled our tent. Chilling thought. Never occurred to us—fire could have trapped us there like Gobby.

One close call after another.

But we get there, get showered. A text bings.

Not over yet. Still by side of road.

I call them.

"All their trucks are in Idaho tonight. They can't help. I finally told them I work for the company and that there'll be a review, but they still offer no satisfaction even though it's 2 a.m.

"Is there anything I can do to help?"

"No, thanks—we'll figure something out."

A text ping awakens me an hour later:

"Things are okay."

•••

Next morning, squeaky clean and well rested, Ro and I decompress as we pack.

I hold up my crumpled fishing license.

"Never even put a line in the water. Deliberately, that is. And look!"

I pull out a pale blue folding fan.

"Whadja bring that for?"

"I thought I'd use on horseback if it got hot."

We laugh so hard we have to reapply our lipstick.

Jim and Jack join us all for breakfast. Don fills us all in.

"We finally realized it was a tire problem, so we called a twenty-four hour tire service. This jolly, mighty young twenty-two-year-old guy came out, got to work, whistling. Whistling at 3 a.m. Replaced the tire. I asked him to check the other one. Lucky he did. Crawled under there and pulled out hunks of shredded tire caught in the axle. Thing mighta snapped."

The final close call of the trip.

Some last laughs, then we give each other the depth of goodbyes survivors give each other, only deeper because it's family, too.

We all make our planes, exhausted but safe.

•••

Returning to New York, I change planes in Minneapolis. Flying in, I spot the stately concrete dome of the Washburn water tower, the green meandering of Tangletown. I land at the airport, next to Fort Snelling, where Dad and Mom are buried.

During my layover, I eat a whopping Glad-To-Be-Alive hot fudge sundae. I indulge as well in the luxury of retrospect. I think about enduring cold, hunger, and dirt, like our ancestors. I reflect on philosophical and entertaining talks around the campfire, a resurrection of the old dining room table. I remember our hands gripping through The Stone of Accord, how even in fear and discomfort and exhaustion, there were no arguments, no pettiness, just people at their best, working together, uniting in adversity, hilarity, affection, love.

Family *in* a landscape, not a house.

Blood and values, handed down. Refined. Spreading mysteriously to those we encounter. A cowboy in a white hat. A miracle of loaves and fruit. Truth writes stories even fiction can't believe. Including the call Jack got as we were parting.

"Someone found Dooley! He's safe and sound, waiting at the vet's."

An hour later, high above the Midwest prairie, it dawned on me that for all my chickenheartedness and griping and quaking, I was breathing easier. Easier than ever, in fact. As if a millstone strapped to my chest since childhood had been left on a rocky riverbank in the backcounty.

We are most vulnerable in childhood, at the mercy of forces beyond our control.

Wilderness can make us feel just as vulnerable, but here childish habits are useless.

You can't please the wilderness. You can't entertain it. You can't lie to it. You can't compete with it. You can't get its attention or its admiration. These efforts are immaterial to its glorious collection of natural processes, whose by-products are staggering beauty, physical challenge, bone-chilling fear, heart. Happily, you can't disappoint the wilderness, either.

The trials and tribs of wilderness? You can't take them personally. It's no use resenting a storm. Or carrying an itchy bag of irritation because a trail defied your expectations. It's just not practical. You simply adapt as best you can, and marvel.

You learn that being afraid is nothing to be afraid of. It comes and goes as naturally as the rush and ripple of the river. You learn to seek not attention, but attentiveness. Not a bad approach to family life. The real prize of the wild is perspective.

Like family, the wilderness requires participation and cooperation. It rewards with communion, beyond the tingle of DNA shared with parents and siblings and other humans. We can feel our relatives in the family of cellular life, life here on Earth: physicality powered by the joy of being. We can feel life trusting itself.

The indoors can't contain this awareness, any more than our bodies can contain all we are as humans. Wilderness embosses this in us.

Gifts of Family

So many gifts to thank my family for.

Your neighbor girl can give you a red squeeze coin purse, or your class give you a card, but it's not your birthday till you come home and smell cake baking and every room they say Go Away I'm wrapping your gift, heart fluttery what did they get you go outside on snowy steps feel how it feels to be older. Then Dad's home martini shaker shaking and "Dinner" calls Mom and on the table red roast beef green beans with almonds and not Christmas fruitcake this time because of Christmas Eve tomorrow, but real black chocolate cake with your name on in yellow and huge pile of presents they pull out your chair sing happy birthday.

Unwrap. Yay! Paint-by-number horses from Pogo-Bogo. Yay! Silver Scottie pin from Kako. Boo! Green eraser from Jim. But don't let him know. Yay! Paddle with cowboy and red ball to-whackit to-whackit from Skip. Yay! Glider plane of ice cream cone type wood from Tom. Yay! Automatic pencil from Ro.

Big one from Mom and Dad. Go slow or it's over too fast. Over your neck curl the gold ribbon, unstick tape from tissue, slide out box. Who could believe my eyes? Jon Gnagy's Learn To Draw Set! My heart's desire! Yay! Yay! Leap up and kiss everyone. Then dinner. Then brothers turn off every light and everyone sings by white flame candles, Happy Birthday to You. Wish for your horse blow out candles everything's dark everyone's clapping. Lights fly on candletips black smell the wax pull one out lick the frosting on it off it. Get surprised how fast it was. Almost you remember it before it happened.

Anniversary

Nearly a year to the day from when we walk out of the wilderness, family gathers again.

Tom and Jim and Ro and I. Spouses Linda, Mark, and my husband. Tom's sons Don and David. Lauren and Derek couldn't make it, but David's kids Sarah and Kaden are here. All three of Jim's boys: Jack, Daniel, and Mike, Jolyne, toddler Creighton, and their new baby daughter Johanna. Ro's son Jackson and his girl. In yet another place of beauty and wildness (albeit one we drive to), we are sharing food and wine and laughter and love and grace and words and the tears words bring.

Together we hike into the woods until a spot claims us. From his backpack, Mark removes the heavy velvet bag, and from the bag, the box. Ro takes it from him.

She and Jim and I leave the family standing watch on the trail, walk off into the trees. This Ponderosa pine feels right. Like children in the backyard, we dig a hole beneath its branches.

Ro opens the box, loosens the bag within and gracefully spirals our brother John's ashes into the hole. A soft gray nest.

We quietly, carefully fill the hole, scattering branches and needles over it, to match the rest of the untouched forest floor. John is now part of the landscape he loved.

Panorama's Edge

A family is a landscape of its own, as granted as the earth and trees:
a wild ecology of feelings, unique in balance, particular of circulation.
Each person, each event becomes environment, familiar and dear
and scary.

Each element's essential in a landscape: none moved, removed
without a subtle or a drastic change. No force shies from the landscape—
all times and changes carried off by elemental forces which transform
the hardest substances to soft.

Patterns marked in rock, in soil, in surface of the sea give a
landscape its identity. Emotion is the weather of the family, patterning
the faces, the voices, and the hearts.

•••

Questions move us through a landscape.

What happened to us?

My brother who cut himself out of the family scrapbook
intermittently repastes himself, aligning with some of us, not
with others.

My brother who was hamstrung in hierarchy freed himself, runs a
business he enjoys, tends his health and family with loving care.

My brother who was committed and released is now released
from life.

My brother crippled by pain endures it still, but travels even to the
wilderness, loving his family, loving his God.

My sister who suffered and drank put down the glass some
forty years ago, now wanders the path my mother, Aunt Irene, and
Gobby took.

My sister who trembled in fear now grounds herself in Spirit,
family, creativity.

I, who ate and ate, healed my compulsion, lovingly tend body and
husband, and am a sometime freelance mother to children, friends,
strangers, animals, plants, objects.

•••

Questions move us through a landscape.

What are the movies? What is TV? Dolls, not babies. Mirrors, not
faces. They trick us when we're young, but we outgrow them. Their
finest insights aren't our own. Go out and feel it for yourself, I say.

What is America? Landscape of millions of landscapes.

And Earth? Family dissolves its borders, for every human shares its
intimate intensity and personal eternity.

•••

As it is being's purpose to cause and fathom meaning, and nature's
purpose to cause and fathom creatures, it's human's purpose to cause
and fathom feeling. Family plunges us into our purpose.

•••

Can we forgive each other for the damage that we suffered
and inflicted?

Questions move us through a landscape. Naturally our viewpoint
changes as we move.

Kin, clan, folk, family, unite in space, in time, in face and body.
The sap in my veins is yours. Its rush of growth we shared. In us
nine immediate hearts were mixed, nine daily urgencies in bare
unconsciousness expressed; nine ways of wanting and behavior. Nine
flavors, nine textures, nine beings now expanded into fourteen more.
Thank you all and all the ones to come.

One day you see a landscape and you ask about the light. Light
makes a landscape visible, lends it harmony, shines impartially.

Love is the light on the family landscape.

Love is not, however, what I thought it was.

It is not a set of reflexes: agreement, pity, gratitude jerking in all circumstances. Love's what is appropriate this moment.

Any act but violence can be an act of love: to listen or to turn away, to dispense or to withhold, to agree, to disagree, to laugh or not to laugh, to be silent or to speak. Love is the attentive ear awaiting the next direction. Love is the next expression of itself.

In that changing light, I view our landscape in a hundred styles, a thousand colors: impeccably Dutch days, clear, precise, and orderly, the light of reason illuminating the domestic scenery; us rosy-cheeked in the light of Rembrandt, gathered at the dining room table, breathless with intellectual wrestling, Dad's pipe glowing; writhing with growth like Van Gogh, pushing each other, defining our vibrating spaces; furious Kandinsky; the illness and despair of Munch. Norman Rockwell does us at the Lake, golden weather on us, high June skies, tether ball and minnow buckets, salted nut rolls. We are sketching, catching frogs, etching scars on ladies in the magazines. Hopper casts his long light through our kitchen. And just now Remington has swept his brush across Montana.

The frontier is right beyond the frame.

Acknowledgments

Profound thanks to the journals and anthologies who first published selections from this book. Anyone who reads or runs a literary magazine keeps us alive.

The Hook In The Heart, first published online in Compass Rose.

Measures Taken, first published online by Carbon Culture.

A version of *Creating My Reality* appears as "BFF" in the volume "Back to High School," published by 650: Where Writers Read.

A version of *Crime on the Catechism* appears in the volume "On Siblings" published by 650: Where Writers Read.

I offer particular gratitude to my brilliant, gentle, experienced, intuitive guide and primary editor on this book: the marvelous memoirist Laura Shaine Cunningham. Rich ongoing conversations, emails, and time spent with her at The Memoir Institute in Stone Ridge, New York, renewed my faith in this project and helped turn recalcitrant pages into the finished book you hold.

Warmest thanks to my beloved and steadfast agent, Anne Marie O'Farrell, whose belief in my work has meant the world to me. Thanks also to her savvy partner Denise Marcil and all the staff at Marcil-O'Farrell Literary Agency for great suggestions and support. Editor Brenda Knight, publisher Chris McKenney, designer Morgane Leoni, and all the Mango team have been wonderful. Without them, this book would not exist. Special thanks wing their way to Molly Friedrich.

Thanks to these small but mighty organizations: The Garrison Art Center in Garrison, New York, The Butterfield Library in Cold Spring, New York, Calling All Poets in New Paltz, New York, and Poets and Writers in NYC, who offered a place and/or funding to explore the early stages of this work.

Writing thrives on friendship. For years of wonderful conversations and support, thank you to Jean Marzollo (sorely missed) and dear Patricia Adams. Dear Tracy Strong, thanks for the best possible local sistering. Hats off to Mark Lacko for design expertise, photography, and friendship, as well as mending my dictionary stand. I am so grateful for the juicy talks, literary and otherwise, with dear Richard Kollath and his partner Ed McCann. Their Creation 650: Where Writers Read is a gift to writers and audiences alike. Thanks to Bill and Ann Strohmeier, to Scott Laughead, Jorie Latham, Vay David, Thomas Donahue, Mark Rettman, and Steve and Cecile Lindstedt for always fanning creative flames. Thanks, Gretchen Dykstra, for incisive advice. Kathy Curto, I'm loving this shared ride with you. Jenna Zark, your passion for this book has helped propel it here. Moira O'Keefe, you gave an early version of this book a big boost, and I'll never forget it.

Thanks also to the remarkable folk who paddled the Flathead with me.

Robin O'Brien, your unflagging support and love are indispensable. As are yours, Jim O'Brien and Dan O'Brien. (Mark Muenster, Linda O'Brien, and Maggie Norman O'Brien will always have my appreciation for caring for my sibs with so much love.)

A wilderness-size bouquet of gratitude to my husband John, ever-darling, John Pielmeier, whose ongoing love, patience, and exquisite literary taste make my creative life possible and my daily life glorious.

About the Author

Irene O'Garden has won or been nominated for prizes in nearly every writing category from stage to e-screen, hardcovers, and children's books, as well as literary magazines and anthologies. Her critically-acclaimed play *Women On Fire* (Samuel French), starring Judith Ivey, played sold-out houses at Off-Broadway's Cherry Lane Theatre and was nominated for a Lucille Lortel Award. Her latest play, *Little Heart*, about artist Corita Kent, won her a Berilla Kerr Playwriting Fellowship and was awarded full development at the New Harmony Play Project.

O'Garden was awarded a Pushcart Prize for her lyric essay "Glad to Be Human" (Untreed Reads). Harper published her first memoir *Fat Girl*, and Nirala Press recently published her book *Fulcrum, Selected Poems*, which contains her prizewinning poem "Nonfiction." "Morning Coffee" recently won the Scott Meyer Award. Her poems and essays have been featured in dozens of literary journals and award-winning anthologies (including *A Slant of Light*, winner of the USA Book Award for Best Anthology), and she has been honored with an Alice Desmond Award and an Oppenheimer for her children's books.

O'Garden has appeared at top literary venues: including The Player's Club, The National Arts Club, the Bowery Poetry Club, the Nuyorican Poetry Café, and KGB in Manhattan; The Poetry Café, Mycenae House, and Vinyl Deptford in London; and recently in Jerusalem. She's a regular contributor to 650: Where Writers Read in Manhattan and Sarah Lawrence College, and she has received several grants from Poets and Writers. O'Garden has lived joyfully with her husband John Pielmeier for forty years. Most known for his play *Agnes of God,* John also writes movies, miniseries, and novels (*Hook's Tale*, Scribner). His stage adaptation of *The Exorcist* ran in London's West End (2017–18) and opens in 2019 in New York.

Represented by Marcil-O'Farrell Literary LLC
c/o Anne Marie O'Farrell
annemarie@marcilofarrellagency.com
516-365-6029

CPSIA information can be obtained
at www.ICGtesting.com
Printed in the USA
BVHW031337070119
537113BV00003BA/5/P

9 781633 538870